MW01178735

HIS WORDS, MY REFLECTIONS

By
Clem D. Chapple

TEACH Services, Inc.
Brushton, New York

Copyright © 2007 TEACH Services, Inc.
ISBN-13: 978-1-57258-470-9
ISBN-10: 1-57258-470-X
Library of Congress Control Number: 2007925562

Published by

TEACH Services, Inc.
www.TEACHServices.com

DEDICATION

This book is dedicated to the loving memory of my husband, Pastor Howard M. Chapple, Sr., who supported me in all of my endeavors. To my children: Howard M. Jr. (Machelle), Christopher (Cosandra), and Bernice. Grandchildren: Howard III, Christina, Angel, Chris Jr., Monisha, Bria, and Tyrin. Great-grandchildren: Synterika, and Syntachia. My siblings Opal Evans, Eddie Dansberry, Jr. (Winnie), and Ernestine Hardy.

This book started out as a legacy for my children. It was written as a voice, from Mama with spiritual advice. In years to come, they will be able to turn to this book and find God's Word, the peace that it brings, and the reflections from their Mama. However, it turned out, that by the grace of God, not only will my children read this book, but perhaps many of my family, friends, co-workers, and hopefully people I do not even know. My prayer is, that each person that reads the pages of this book, will come away, with a greater desire to spend more time with Jesus, because after all, He is the one we will spend eternity with.

CONTENTS

Chapter 1

AFFLICTIONS,
TODAY IS THE DAY OF SALVATION,
STRONG IN FAITH,
BE NOT UNEQUALLY YOKED TOGETHER,
BE YE HOLY,
A PURPOSED HEART.

AFFLICTIONS

"For our light afflictions which is but for a moment, worketh for us a far more exceeding and eternal weight of glory, While we look not at the things which are seen, but at the things which are not seen: For the things which are seen are temporal; but the things which are not seen are eternal" (II Corinthians 4:17, 18).

These troubles and sufferings of ours are, after all, quite small and won't last very long. Yet this short time of distress will result in God's richest blessings upon us forever and ever. So we do not look at what we can see right now, the troubles all around us, but we look forward to the joys in heaven which we have not seen. The troubles will soon be over but the joys to come will last forever. "For I reckon that the sufferings of this present time are not worthy to be compared with the glory which shall be revealed in us". (Romans 8:18). What we suffer now is nothing compared to the glory He will give us later. "But it is written, Eye hath not seen, nor ear heard, neither have entered into the heart of man, the things which God hath prepared for them that love Him" (I Corinthians 2:9).

TODAY IS THE DAY OF SALVATION

"For He saith, I have heard thee in a time accepted, and in the day of salvation have I succoured thee: behold, now is the accepted time; behold now is the day of salvation" (II Corinthians 6:2).

God says when the time came, I listened to you, and when you needed help I came to your rescue. This is the day for you to be saved yesterday is gone, tomorrow is not promised. To day, this minute is all that you have. The devil has deceived us into believing that we can come to God at our own time. He tells us we need to stop all our sinning before we can come to God. However, this is the main reason to come to God. For Him to save us from our sin. He can help us. The word says: " No man can come to me, except the father which hath sent me draw him: and I will raise him up at the last day". (John 6:44). At this time of confusion our prayer should be: "But as for me, my prayer is to thee, O Lord. At an acceptable time, O God in the abundance of thy steadfast love answer me". (Psalms 69:13).

STRONG IN FAITH

"And being not weak in faith, he considered not his own body now dead, when he was about a hundred years old , neither yet the deadness of Sara's womb; He staggered not at the promise of God through unbelief, but was strong in faith, giving glory to God" (Romans 4:19, 20).

Abraham did not let his mind think about his body, his reproduction organs, now dead, as well as Sara's. He gave God all the glory, knowing that all things were possible with God. His faith was strong in God's power. In our problems today, whether there be sickness, grief, loneliness, or poverty, we must not think about them, but think about God. "Now unto Him that is able to do exceeding abundantly above all that we ask or think, according to the power that worketh in us" (Ephesians 3:20). Our glory should be to God who by His mighty power at work in us is able to do far more than we would ever dare to ask or even dream of infinitely beyond our highest prayers, desires, thoughts, or hopes.

BE NOT UNEQUALLY YOKED TOGETHER

"Be ye not unequally yoked together with unbelievers: for what fellowship hath righteousness with unrighteous: and what communion hath darkness with light?" (II Corinthians 6:14)

Marriage of believers and unbelievers has been a snare by which satan has captured many earnest souls, who thought they could win the unbeliever, but most cases have themselves drifted away from the faith into doubt, backsliding, and loss of religion. God warned Israel constantly, "Give not your daughters unto their son's, neither take their daughters unto your sons, nor seek their peace or their wealth for ever" (Ezra 9:12). Even Solomon fell before the influence of heathen wives. "His wives turned away his heart after other god;s" (I Kings 11:4). No christian can marry an unbeliever without running serious risk, and placing himself upon the enemy's ground. The scripture does not condone separation after the union has been formed. (I Corinthians 7:2–16). But common sense should teach us that faith can best be maintained, and domestic happiness best ensured, where both husband and wife are believers, and of the same faith.

BE YE HOLY

"Wherefore gird up the lions of your mind, be sober, and hope to the end for the grace that is to be brought unto you at the revelation of Jesus Christ. As obedient children, not fashioning yourselves according to the former lusts in your ignorance: But He which hath called you is Holy, so be ye holy, in all manner of conversation; Because it is written, be ye holy; for I am Holy" (I Peter 1:13–16).

We must prepare our minds for action, be self-controlled; set your hope fully on the grace to be given you when Jesus Christ is revealed. Don't slip back into your old ways, doing evil because you knew no better. Be just as He who called you is Holy. We are called to be holy, therefore, it must be an attainable goal; otherwise why would the bible more than once call us to holiness? Holiness basically means to be set apart for God's use. This scripture is dealing with our lusts and passions. However, we are to be holy in all manner of conduct, behavior, and lifestyle. Though we have been given these basic desires by God, we are to separate from the world and the world's indulgences, abuses and perversions of these desires. (*Quarterly* July–Sept 2005).

A PURPOSED HEART

"But Daniel purposed in his heart that he would not defile himself with the portion of the King's meat, nor with the wine which he drank: therefore he requested of the prince of the eunuchs that he might not defile himself" (Daniel 1:8).

Nebuchadnezzar attacked Jerusalem, he ordered Ashpenaz, chief of eunuch, to bring along to Babylon, young men of the royal family. Young men with no blemish, who were skilful in wisdom, cunning in knowledge, understanding science and qualified to serve in the King's palace. Among these young men were Daniel, Hananiah, Mishael, and Azariah. The King wanted them to eat the same food that he ate, and drink the wine that he drank. But Daniel didn't want to defile himself with the Kings food. Daniel wanted to "Obey God rather than man" (Acts 5:29). Therefore, he asked the prince of the eunuchs to give them vegetables and water for ten days and he would see that they would be healthier than the young men that ate from the King's table. God gave the eunuch compassion for Daniel and he agreed to the test. After ten days Daniel and his friends looked healthier and better nourished than the others. Because Daniel wanted to honor God by not defiling his body; God gave them knowledge, skill in learning, wisdom, and to Daniel he gave the understanding of all visions and dreams.

Chapter 2

BEFORE THEY CALL I WILL ANSWER, THINK ON THESE THINGS, GOD OF COMFORT, SEEK PEACE, PRAYER FOR PETER, MEANINGFUL LABOR.

BEFORE THEY CALL I WILL ANSWER

"And it shall come to pass that before they call I will answer, and while they are yet speaking, I will hear" (Isaiah 65:24).

Nothing catches God by surprise. He knows everything. When we pray and ask God for a particular thing, or work out a situation; He has already taken care of the matter. He knew that when you were born, there would be a need on that day and He took care of the provision at that time. He has the answer. He is just waiting for us to ask. "Ask and it shall be given you; seek, and ye shall find; knock, and it shall be opened unto you: For everyone that asketh receiveth; and he that seeketh findeth; and to him that knocketh it shall be opened" (Matthew 7:7). When we have problems we try to work them out ourselves. After we wrestle and wrestle and still don't find the answer, we turn to God as a last resort. And He always provides the provision. "He shall call upon me, and I will answer him: I will be with him in trouble; I will deliver him, and honour him. With long life will I satisfy him, and shew him my salvation" (Psalms 91:15, 16).

THINK ON THESE THINGS

"Finally,bretheren , whatsoever things are true, whatsoever things are honest, whatsoever things are just, whatsoever things are pure, whatsoever things are lovely, whatsoever things are of good report ; If there be any virtue, and if there be any praise, think on these things" (Philippians 4:8).

Most of the time when we see flaws in our character, we desire to change them. We believe we should work on that particular behavior. This should not be the case. We should ask God to sanctify our thoughts and think on true, honest, and just things. Thoughts become things. We must talk to ourselves and see ourselves as the person we desire to be. Once our thoughts reflect what we genuinely want to become, the appropriate emotions and the behavior will happen automatically. In the book of Numbers, Moses sent out spies to search the land of Canaan that the Lord had given to the children of Israel. Moses sent out twelve men and they came back with this report: "And they told him, and said, We came unto the land whither thou sentest us, and surely it floweth with milk and honey; and this is the fruit of it. Nevertheless the people be strong that dwell in the land, and the cities are walled, and very great: and moreover we saw the children of Anak there. And they brought up an evil report of the land which they had searched unto the children of Israel, saying, The land, through which we have gone to search it, is a land that eateth up the inhabitants thereof; and all the people that we saw in it are men of a great stature" (Numbers 13:27, 28, 32). Disbelief is an evil report. Whenever we doubt the power of God in any situation, it is an evil report. Let us trust in God's word and think on honest, just, pure, lovely, and things of good report and be blessed.

GOD OF COMFORT

"Blessed be God, even the Father of our Lord Jesus Christ, the father of mercies, and the God of all comfort; who comforteth us in all our tribulation, that we may be able to comfort them which are in any trouble, by the comfort wherwith we ourselves are comforted of God" (II Corinthians 1:3, 4).

Many times troubles, sickness, and grief come into our lives and we complain to God. We ask why did this happen? However, we should be saying, God, what do I need to learn from this trial? God wants to enable us to comfort someone else that will go through the same trial. "He shall not be afraid of evil tidingss: his heart is fixed, trusting in the Lord" (Psalms 112:7). Each trial makes us stronger and stronger. "My brethren, count it all joy when ye fall into divers temptations; Knowing this, that the trying of your faith worketh patience. But let patience have her perfect work, that ye may be perfect and entire, wanting nothing" (James 1:2–4). When our lives are full of difficulties and temptations and our way seem dark, our patience has a chance to grow. We shouldn't try to squirm out of our problems, because when our patience is in full bloom, then we will be ready for anything, strong in character, full and complete. Then we are truly able to comfort others, assuring them that God will bring them through.

SEEK PEACE

"And seek the peace of the city whither I have caused you to be carried away captives, and pray unto the Lord for it: for in the peace thereof shall ye have peace" (Jeremiah 29:7).

Jeremiah wrote to the elders who had been carried off to Babylon, by Nebuchadnezzar as captives. The Lord told them to build homes, dwell in them, plant garden, eat the fruit of them, and multiply yourselves, that you don't diminish. One of the most important things that God told them was to seek peace of the city by working for the prosperity of Babylon. He told them to pray for the people that took them as captives. This was not an easy thing to do. They didn't have the whole bible as we do, that tell us to "Pray for those who despitefully use you" (Matthew 5:44). This scripture lets us know, that no matter what negative situation we find ourselves in, we should pray for the person or persons, who caused this particular situation. He also said, in the peace of Babylon, you shall also have peace. What a wonderful truth! If only we could grasp this truth, how different our lives would be.

Remember Job? "And the Lord turned the captivity of Job, when he prayed for his friends; also the Lord gave Job twice as much as he had before" (Job 42:10).

PRAYER FOR PETER

"And the Lord said Simon, Simon, behold, satan hath desired to have you, that he may sift you as wheat : But I have prayed for thee, that thy faith fail not; and when thou art converted, strengthen thy brethren" (Luke 22:31, 32).

Jesus prayed for Peter that his faith would not fail. Some of us look at this scripture and believe that Peter failed. I believed God answered Jesus prayer. I don't believe that Peter failed, loosing a battle dosen't mean we have lost the war. God dosen't see us as failures, just learners. When Peter was converted, he did a great work for God's service. He preached the spirit-empowered sermon at Pentecost to the assembled Jews, he and John healed the lame man (Acts 2:14:3, 2), he was used to expose the sin of Ananias and Sapphira (Acts 5:1–12), He exposed the unworthy motives of Simon, the sorcerer (Acts 8:14–24, healed Aeneas, and raised Dorcas from the dead (Acts 9:32–43). Peter's love for Christ molded him into a man of stability, humility, and he accomplished courageous service for God, becoming one of the noble pillars of the church.

MEANINGFUL LABOR

"And the Lord God took the man, and put him into the garden of Eden to dress it and to keep it" (Genesis 2:15).

Meaningful labor for the human family was part of God's original and perfect plan. A portion of Adams and eve's time was to be spent in the happy employment of dressing the garden. Their labor was not wearisome but pleasant and invigorating. God created us with a desire to work. Most of us have some activities that we enjoy doing. An activity brings satisfaction to the person, when the labor is in harmony with the way God created that person. Unfortunately, in our fallen state; only a few know themselves well enough, to really understand what God created them for. With the lack of a secure identity in Christ, many of us settle for jobs that do not give us enjoyment. When we love ourselves the way God loves us, we are equipped to make choices in line with God's will for our lives. (*Quartely* July–Sept. 2005).

Chapter 3

THE LORD IS ON MY SIDE,
PRIDE GOETH BEFORE DESTRUCTION,
THE INCORRUPTIBLE CROWN,
DELIGHT THYSELF ALSO IN THE LORD.

THE LORD IS ON MY SIDE

"The Lord is on my side; I will not fear: what can man do unto me?" (Psalms 118:6).

God is for me, how can I be afraid of what mere man can do to me. The Lord is on my side! These six words should relieve all fears. Since God is on our side He wants the best for us. When we believe in God's word, the Lord won't allow anything to happen to us except what is His will for our lives. However, sometimes the things He allows may cause us to be fearful, but we must trust Him and know that He never makes mistakes. We must believe that it will work out for our good. "And we know that all things work together for good to them that love God, to them who are called according to His purpose" (Romans 8:28). As we love God and fit into His plans, we have nothing to fear.

PRIDE GOETH BEFORE DESTRUCTION

"Pride goeth before destruction, and a haughty spirit before a fall" (Proverbs 16:18).

False pride keeps us from admitting to others that our attitude and actions have been wrong. Pride gives us a false sense of values and it closes to us the door to the blessed life. Pride tells us that we are self- sufficient and destroys our humility. And God's power is blocked from us. "When pride cometh, then cometh shame: but with the lowly is wisdom"

(Proverbs 11:2). An example of: "pride before destruction" is seen in the book of Jeremiah. Johanan and the army captains and all the people, came to Jeremiah and asked him to pray and ask the Lord to show us what to do and where to go? They said, "May the curse of God be on us if we refuse to obey whatever He says we should do". Jeremiah prayed and ten days later the Lord answered him. The Lord said, "If you will still abide in this land, then will I build you, and not pull you down, and I will plant you, and not pluck you up: for I repent me of the evil that I have done unto you. Be not afraid of the king of Babylon, of whom ye are afraid; be not afraid of him, saith the Lord: for I am with you to save you, and to deliver you from his hand" (Jeremiah 42:1–16). The Lord said if you refuse to obey me and insist on going to Egypt, the war and famine you fear, will follow you there, and you will perish. When Jeremiah had finished, "Then spake Azariah the son of Hoshaiah, and Johanan the son of Kareah, and all the proud men, saying unto Jeremiah, Thou speakest falsely: the Lord our God hath not sent thee to say, Go not into Egypt to sojourn there" (Jeremiah 43:2). They refused to obey the Lord and all of them started off for Egypt where they perished.

THE INCORRUPTIBLE CROWN

"Know ye not that they which run in a race run all, but one receiveth the prize? So run, that ye may obtain. And every man that striveth for the mastery is temperate in all things. Now they do it to obtain a corruptible crown; but we an incorruptible" (I Corinthians 9:24, 25).

Everyone who competes in the race goes into strict training. They do it to get a crown that will not last; but we do it to receive a crown that will last forever. In this race, we deny ourselves, doing things that we do not always feel like doing. Such as bible study, praying, and witnessing. The same as the runners, they must eat right, get enough sleep, and run. "I press toward the mark for the prize of the high calling of God in Christ Jesus" (Philippians 3:14). We strain to reach the end of the race to receive that incorruptible crown, eternal life.

Their prize is temporal, it will be forgotten, tarnished, and the money spent, and only one can win that prize. But the prize we are striving for can be won by as many that choose to endure until the end. "Henceforth there is laid up for me a crown of righteousness, which the Lord, the righteous judge, shall give me at that day: and not to me only, but unto all them also that love His appearing" (II Timothy 4:8). And that prize is eternal life.

DELIGHT THYSELF ALSO IN THE LORD

"Delight thyself also in the Lord and He shall give thee the desires of thine heart" (Psalms 37:4).

What a wonderful promise! It isn't very hard to delight in the one, who has loved us so much, that He gave the best that He had, that we might be brought back to Him, and have a choice to spend eternity with Him. "My sheep hear my voice, and I know them, and they follow me: And I give unto them eternal life; and they shall never perish, neither shall any man pluck them out of my hand" (John 10:27, 28). We may think this is too good to be true, but we must understand what it means to "Delight thyself also in the Lord". We all like to spend time with the person we really love, don't we? So if we really want to delight ourselves in the Lord, we must spend time in His word, obey His commandments, pray, and witness to others. When we love the Lord, we love His people, too. When we do these things, our love grows and grows. We began to take on His character. We say the things He says and do the things He does. At this point the Lord can give us the desires of our hearts, because we will only ask for things that He will be happy to give us, as we abide in Him. The things we ask for will glorify Him and be a blessing to our family and those around us. "If ye abide in me, and my words abide in you, ye shall ask what ye will, and it shall be done unto you" (John 15:7)

Chapter 4

CHOOSE DEATH OR LIFE

CHOOSE DEATH OR LIFE

"Death and life are in the power of the tongue: and they that love it shall ear the fruit there of" (Proverbs 18:21).

Your tongue can be used to bring healing, prosperity, love, joy, and life to you. Or, it can be used to bring poverty, sickness, sadness, and death. It all depends upon the words that are in our hearts. "This book of the law shall not depart out of thy mouth, but thou shalt meditate therein day and night, that thou mayest observe to do according to all that is written therein: for then thou shalt make thy way prosperous, and then thou shalt have good success" (Joshua 1:8). The Lord told Joshua to mediate on His word. In His word is everything we need for life. "My son, attend to my words, incline thine ear unto my sayings. Let them not depart from thine eyes; keep them in the midst of thine heart. For they are life unto those that find them, and health to all their flesh" (Proverbs 4:20–22). The word that is kept before our eyes and in our heart will give healing and eternal life.

Chapter 5

LIFE MORE ABUNDANTLY,
HE SHALT HAVE WHATSOEVER HE SAITH,
BE CONTENT.

LIFE MORE ABUNDANTLY

"The thief cometh not, but for to steal, and to kill, and to destroy: I am come that they might have life, and that they might have it more abundantly" (John 10:10).

All of God's promises to His children were stolen by the devil in the Garden of Eden. He stole eternal life, prosperity, and healing. He gave us death, sickness, and poverty. But God, who loved us so much, sent His only begotten Son, to ransom us back. Jesus restored eternal life, prosperity, and healing. The devil knows that the victory is ours in Christ Jesus, but there are many that do not know. "For whatsoever is born of God overcometh the world: and this is the victory that overcometh the world, even our faith. Who is he that overcometh the world, but he that believeth that Jesus is the Son of God" (I John 5:4, 5). Therefore, we must be about our Father's business. Telling others about the "Good News that whosoever is born of God has the victory". Because Jesus came, He made it possible for us to be free from death: "Jesus said unto her, I am the resurrection, and the life: he that believeth in me, though he were dead, yet shall he live: and whosoever liveth and believeth in me shall never die. Believest thou this?" (John 11:25, 26).

HE SHALT HAVE WHATSOEVER HE SAITH

"And Jesus answering saith unto them, have faith in God, for verily I say unto you, that whosoever shall say unto this mountain, be thou removed, and be thou cast into the sea and shall not doubt in his heart, but shall believe that those things

14

which he saith shall come to pass; he shall have whatsoever he saith. Therefore I say unto you what things soever ye desire, when ye pray, believe that ye recieve them, and ye shall have them" (Mark 11:22–24).

The verse says. "Whosoever shall say unto this mountain, be thou removed, and be thou cast into the sea and shall not doubt in his heart" The mouth and the heart (mind) must agree. The mind must believe what the mouth is saying. When we claim this promise in prayer, we must not doubt in our hearts. We must believe that we shall have the thing at the time we pray. By faith we must believe that we shall have it at God's timing. So what will we do as we end our prayer? If I believe that by faith, I shall receive it, I will say thank you Lord, I believe that I shall receive it. From this point on we will be in a spirit of thanks because of our faith in God. We must have faith "In God" When the woman with the issue of blood was healed, Jesus said, "Thy faith hath made thee whole" Jesus let her know her faith in Him had made her whole. Jesus gives us all a measure of faith. (Romans 12:3). This faith is to know, that He has all power and that nothing, is too hard for Him. The more that we began to trust in Him, the more our faith will grow and all doubt will be removed from our minds and we will have whatever we say.

BE CONTENT

"But I rejoice greatly, that now at the last your care of me hath flourished again; wherein ye were also careful, but lacked opportunity. Not that I speak in respect of want: for I have learned, in whatsoever state I am, therewith to be content" (Philippians 4:10, 11).

Paul was letting the people know, how happy he was to, receive help from them again. But he let them know, that he had gotten along well without their help. Because he had learned to live with what he had. Paul had learned to be content in every situation by depending on God's help. We must first of all accept the situation we are in, knowing that God has allowed it to happen. After accepting we must seek God to find out if there is anything we can do along with prayer. If there is nothing else we can do, we must endure until God sees fit to deliver us. The word tells us that: "But godliness with contenment is great gain. For we brought nothing into this world, and it is certain we can carry nothing out" (I Timothy 6:6, 7). To be truly rich is to be godly and content with what we have. We must always remember, that if we are walking with Christ that whatever happens in our life He will work it out for our good. (Romans 8:28). When we love God and are fitting into His plan for our life we can be content.

Chapter 6

RECEIVE WITH MEEKNESS THE ENGRAFTED WORD, TRUSTING IN THE LORD.

RECEIVE WITH MEEKNESS THE ENGRAFTED WORD

"Wherefore lay apart all filthiness and superfluity of naughtiness, and receive with meekness the engrafted word, which is able to save your souls" (James 1:21).

We must get rid of all the wrong in our lives and humbly accept the word planted in us, which can save us. "In the beginning was the Word, and the Word was with God, and the Word was God. And the Word was made flesh, and dwelt among us, (and we beheld His glory, the glory as of the only begotten of the Father,) full of grace and truth" (John 1:1,14). Jesus was made flesh and came down to show us how to receive His salvation. As we receive God's word by faith, with humbleness of heart, allowing it to saturate our mind it will drive out evil thoughts, all pretense, and disobedience. "For the word of God is quick, and powerful, and sharper than any two-edged sword, piercing even to the dividing asunder of soul and spirit, and of the joints and marrow, and is a discerner of the thoughts and intents of the heart (Hebrews 4:12). Jesus came to save our souls (people), because souls die. "Behold, all souls are mine, as the soul of the father, so also the soul of the son is mine: the soul that sinneth, it shall die" (Ezekiel 18:4).

TRUSTING IN THE LORD

"He shall not be afraid of evil tiding: his heart is fixed trusting in the Lord" (Psalms 112:7).

When we really trust in the Lord, we won't fear bad news, nor live in dread of what may happen. Because our minds are settled and we believe God will take care of us. We should have the kind of trust that Abraham had, when God told him to offer up his only son, for a burnt offering. Abraham obeyed and what did God say to Abraham, when He knew that Abraham was going to do as He asked? "And He said, lay not thine hand upon the lad, neither do thou any thing unto him: for I know that thou fearest God, seeing thou hast not withheld thy son, thine only son from me" (Genesis 22:12). This is the kind of fear that the Lords wants from us, the fear that is willing to obey no matter what He asks. When we fear God we have no reason to fear anybody else. That is why all through out the scripture the Lord tells us fear not, because as we fear Him only, all needs are met. "Praise ye the Lord, Blessed is the man that feareth the Lord, that delighteth greatly in His commandments, His seed shall be mighty upon earth: the generation of the upright shall be blessed. Wealth and riches shall be in His house: and his righteousness endureth for ever" (Psalms 112:1–3). As we fear God only we are blessed beyond expression, our children are mighty, wealth and riches are in our house.

Chapter 7

CHARITY SUFFERETH LONG,
I WILL PASS OVER YOU.

CHARITY SUFFERETH LONG

"And now abideth faith, hope, charity. These three but the greatest of these is charity" (I Corinthians 13:13).

The word charity means love. Love is the greatest force on the face of the earth. It has been estimated that 70% of all diseases are caused by supressed emotions. Regret, sorrow, and remorse tear down the cells of the body. Thoughts of hate generate a deadly poison in the body which can kill if not neutralized by love. Diseases are caused by the violation of the law of love. Resentment and anger produce sickness and sorrow. Love is an awakener. Psychologist have found that people who know how to express love are healthier, they tend to get sick less and recover more quickly, they age more slowly, have better skin color, clearer skin, better posture and circulation than the depressed, cynical and bitter type of people. Thoughts of love cause beneficial chemical changes to take place in the body. Thoughts of love bring fourth life, even change thoughts of death to thoughts of life, love harmonizes thoughts of the mind bringing peace to both mind and Spirit. Love is so powerful because: "God is love" (John 4:16) Charity suffereth long (love never gives up), charity is kind (love cares more for others than forself), charity envieth not (love does not want what belongs to someone else), charity vaunteth not itself (love does not strut saying, look at me), charity is not puffed up (doesn't have a swelled head), charity doth not behave itself unseemingly (love doesn't force itself on others), charity seeketh not her own (isn't always me first), charity is not easily provoked (love doesn't fly off the handle) charity thinketh no evil (love doesn't keep score of the sin of others), charity rejoiceth not in iniquity (love doesn't delight in evil), charity rejoiceth in the truth (love takes pleasure in truth) charity beareth all things (love put up with anything) charity believeth all things (love trusts God always) charity hopeth all things (love always look for the best) charity endureth all things (love never looks back) charity never faileth (love keeps on going until the end).

I WILL PASS OVER YOU

"For the Lord will pass through to smite the Egyptians; and when He seeth the blood upon the lintel, and the two side posts, the Lord will pass over the door, and will not suffer the destroyer to come in unto your houses to smite you" (Exodus 12:23).

In (Exodus 12:3) the Lord tells Moses and Aaron to tell every man on the tenth day of the month to take a lamb without blemish, a male one year old, and keep it until the fourteenth day and kill it in the evening. Then take the blood and put it on the two side posts and on the upper door post of the houses. Because of the blood of lamb, the Lord passed over the Isarelites. He said, "And when I see the blood, I will pass over you" (Exodus 12:13). If the blood of the lamb was good, how much more powerful is Jesus blood. "But now in Christ Jesus ye who sometimes were far off are made nigh by the blood of Christ" (Ephesians 2:13) Because of the blood, we can be cleansed continually. (I John 7:9), because of the blood we are sanctified. (Hebrew 10:14). Because of the blood a drunkard can be transformed into a sober, sensible individual, sorrow and sadness can be turned into joy and gladness, a woman of the street can be changed into a saint of God, a heart that is cold and hard can become tender and compassionate, failure can be turned into success, bitterness into sweetness, anxiety into assurance, work into pleasure, weakness into strength, and fear into faith. Have you accepted Jesus blood? It was shed for you and for me for the remission of our sins. (Matthew 26:28).

Chapter 8

WE SERVE THE LORD, IDLE WORDS

WE SERVE THE LORD

"Servants, obey in all things your masters according to the flesh; not with eye service, as menpleasers; but in singleness of heart fearing God: And what so ever ye do, do it heartily, as to the Lord, and not unto men; knowing that of the Lord ye shall recieve the reward of the inheritance: for ye serve the Lord Christ" (Colossians 3:22).

The majority of people spend the better part of their life engaged in some form of labor. If this is where most of our time is spent, and where we come into contact with people outside our family and church circles, it is also our greatest witnessing opportunity. According to the way we do our job what impression would people have about our faith? Would they see someone who cares for others or someone concerned with his or her own advancement? Would they see an honest and trustworthy person committed to upholding the value of his or her God, or would they see someone willing to cut corners? Would they see someone committed to offering solutions or someone who spends their time around the water cooler discussing all the problems? Would they see someone easily discouraged or someone with an inner source of strength. Our faith should be seen in our work; we shouldn't just work when the boss is around but all the time. Whatever we do, it should be for the Lord; because we will recieve our rewards from Him. God places His children in certain situations for a reason, let us not lose sight of our greater mission. (*Quartely* Jul–Sept. pg 121, 2005).

IDLE WORDS

"Every idle word that men shall speak, they shall give account there of in the day of judgement. For by thy words thou shalt be justified and by thy words thou shalt be condemned" (Matthew 12:36,37).

Idle words are useless, futile, fruitless, pointless, aimless, empty, vacant and unimportant. Idle words are any words that disagree with the word of God. Our words will justify us or condemn us. Have you ever thought about the words you say during your waking hours? What is your self talk? We carry on a conversation with ourselves all throughout the day. What are we saying? This verse is not only speaking about what we say to others, but also what we say to ourselves. Justified is an act of free grace by which God pardons the sinner and accept him as righteous because of what Christ did at the cross. Faith is the only means of justification. Condemned is having no way out. We were under the law of sin and death, and Christ came and redemned us by giving us a choice to live or die. We are either speaking the words that God says about us or we are speaking satan words. Instead of saying "This is going to be another bad day" say, "This is the day which the Lord has made, we will rejoice and be glad in it" (Psalms 118:24). Don't say, "I am just no good" say, "I will praise thee for I am fearfully and wonderfully made" (Psalms 139:14). How do we stop these idle words? By doing what this verse says, "Finally brethren, whatsoever things are true, whatsoever things are honest, whatsoever things are just, whatsoever things are of good report; if there be any virtue and if there be any praise think on these things" (Philippians 4:8). Before we speak, or think, we should ask ourselves, is what I am about to say or think, true, honest, just, pure, lovely, and of good report? If your answer is yes, your words will not condemn you.

Chapter 9

WHY ARE YOU FEARFUL?,
I AM THAT I AM,
THE PRECIOUS BLOOD OF CHRIST,
SIN HAS HID HIS FACE FROM YOU.

WHY ARE YOU FEARFUL?

"And He arose, and rebuked the wind, and said unto the sea peace, be still. And the wind ceased, and there was a great calm. And He said unto them, why are you so fearful? How is it that you have no faith?" And they feared exceedingly, and said one to another, what manner of man is this, that even the wind and sea obey Him?" (Mark 4: 39–41)

As I read these words, it brings to mind the Psalms which says: "O Lord God of hosts, who is a strong Lord like unto thee? Or to thy faithfulness round about thee? Thou rulest the raging of the sea: when the waves there of arise, thou stillest them" (Psalms 89:8, 9) Jesus was in the boat and the disciples were afraid! Isn't that just like us? Jesus told us: "I will never leave thee, nor forsake thee" (Hebrew 13:5). Jesus asked the question, "How is it that you have no faith?" And He is asking us today the same question. We have no faith because we look at the circumstances instead of looking at Jesus. The mighty one who made the world and every thing in it in six days! Our circumstances can look awful huge sometimes, but we must take our eyes away from the circumstances and look at Jesus, the saviour of the world. We must realize that nothing catches Jesus by surprise, He has already taken care of the situation. Let us understand that Jesus is the captain, He holds the bow that guides the ship and He keeps us on course.

23

I AM THAT I AM

"And Moses said unto God, Behold, when I come unto the children of Israel, and shall say unto them, The God of your fathers hath sent me unto you; and they shall say to me, What is His name? What shall I say unto them? And God said unto Moses, I AM THAT I AM: and He said, Thus shalt thou say unto the children of Israel, I AM hath sent me unto you" (Exodus 3:13, 14).

The Lord is the sovereign God, The God of our ancestors Abraham, Isaac, and Jacob. The angel of the Lord appeared to Moses in a burning bush that was not consumed. God told Moses, first of all to reverence Him by pulling off his shoes, because he was standing on holy ground. He told Moses I have seen the affliction of my people in Egypt and I have come to deliver them. The Lord told Moses, "I am going to send you to deliver them" Moses was very afraid, even after all that the Lord had promised him. To still the fear in Moses God said, "What is that in thine hand? And he said, a rod. And He said, Cast it on the ground. And he cast it on the ground, and it became a serpent; and Moses fled from before it. And the Lord said unto Moses, Put forth thine hand, and take it by the tail. And he put forth his hand, and caught it, and it became a rod in his hand" (Exodus 4:1–3). "Certainly I will be with you." The Lord is the great I AM! He is whatever we need at any time. Jesus said unto them, "Verily, verily, I say unto you. Before Abraham was, I am" (John 8:58). And with the great I AM on our side, we can be, "More than conquerors through Him that loved us" (Romans 8:37).

THE PRECIOUS BLOOD OF CHRIST

"Forasmuch as ye know that ye were not redeemed with corruptible things, as silver and gold, from your vain conversation received by tradition from your fathers; But with the precious blood of Christ as of a lamb without blemish and without spot" (I Peter 1:18, 19).

God paid a ransom to save you, that you might spend eternity with Him. The ransom that He paid was not mere gold or silver, as you know, but He paid for you with the precious blood of Christ the sinless, spotless, lamb of God. "Neither by the blood of goats and calves, but by his own blood He entered in once in the holy place, having obtained eternal redemption for us" (Hebrews 9:12). God chose Jesus for this purpose long before the world began, but only recently was He brought into public view, in the last day, as a blessing to us. Since God has ransomed us back to Him, we must realize that our bodies do not belong to us, but to God. "For ye are bought with a price; therefore glorify God in your body, and in your spirit, which are God's." (I Corinthians 6:20). God has bought you with a great price, He gave us the best that heaven had to offer. So use every part of your body to give glory back to God, because He owns it.

SIN HAS HID HIS FACE FROM YOU

"Behold, the Lord's hand is not shortened, that it cannot save, neither His ear heavy, that it cannot hear. But your iniquities have separated between you and your God, and your sins have hid His face from you, that He will not hear. For your hands are defiled with blood, and your fingers with iniquity; your lips have spoken lies, your tongue hath muttered perverseness" (Isaiah 59:1–3).

God does not hear or answer the prayers of people who are openly and willfully sinning against Him. Isaiah tells the people the Lord is able to save you, and He is not deaf. Your sins have separated you from Him and He has turned His face from you. You don't care about being fair and true. Your lawsuits are based on lies; time is used for plotting evil deeds and doing them. You cheat and short change everyone. Everything you do is evil. Your feet run to do evil and rush to murder; and wherever you go, you leave behind a trail of misery and death. You don't know what true peace is. Does this sounds like todays world? "For men shall be lovers of their own selves, covetous, boasters, proud, blasphemers, disobedient to parents, unthankful, unholy, Without natural affection, trucebreakers, false accusers, incontinent, fierce despisers of those that are good, Traitors, heady, highminded, lovers of pleasures more than lovers of God; Having a form of godliness, but denying the power thereof: from such turn away" (II Timothy 3:2–5). Paul was warning Timothy of these things to come. And it also is a warning to us. We must continue in the word so that we will be able to say as Paul said: "I have fought a good fight, I have finished my course, I have kept the faith: Henceforth there is laid up for me a crown of righteousness, which the Lord the righteous judge, shall give me at that day: and not me only, but unto them also that love His appearing" (II Timothy 4:7, 8).

Chapter 10

NOW FAITH IS,
WALK CIRCUMSPECTLY,
WORSHIP GOD IN THE SPIRIT,
HE SWARE BY HIMSELF.

NOW FAITH IS

"Now faith is the substance of things hoped for, the evidence of things not seen" (Hebrews 11:1).

Faith is the confident assurance that something we want is going to happen. It is the certainty that what we hope for is waiting for us, even though we cannot see it ahead. This verse focuses more on God's promises and the evidence that He has left behind: creation, archaeology, history, and Bible prophecy. Because of the evidence that God has left behind, we believe that heaven does exist, and that God does have a future home for us. "But now they desire a better country, that is, an heavenly: wherefore God is not ashamed to be called their God: for he hath prepared for them a city" (Hebrew 11:16). By faith Abraham offered up Isaac, by faith Moses refused to be called the son of Pharaoh's daughter, by faith the Isarelites passed through the Red sea as by dry land,and by faith the walls of Jericho fell down, "And these all, having obtained a good report through faith, recieved not the promise: God having provided some better thing for us, that they without us should not be made perfect" (Hebrew 11:39, 40). All of them pleased God because of their faith! But still they died without being given what had been promised. This was because God had somehting better in store for us. And He did not want them to reach the goal of their faith without us. Faith is active, enduring, living and indwelling.

WALK CIRCUMSPECTLY

"See then that ye walk circumspectly, not as fools, but as wise, Redeeming the time, because the days are evil. Wherefore be ye not unwise, but understanding what the will of the Lord is" (Ephesians 5:15–17).

Be careful how you act, these are difficult days. Be wise making the best of every opportunity you have for doing good. Therefore do not be vague and thoughtless, but understanding and firmly grasping what the will of the Lord is. Paul is writing to the Ephesians church. He is telling them what is expected of them because they have been called to a new life. Followers of the Lord are God's dear children, and they must follow God's example. You used to live in the dark, but you must now live in the light and make your light shine. "Walk in wisdom toward them that are without, redeeming the time. Let your speech be always with grace, seasoned with salt, that you may know how ye ought to answer every man." (Colossians 4:5, 6) When we are with unbelievers, we should always make good use of the time. We should be pleasant and hold their interest when we speak the message. We should choose our words carefully and be ready to give answers to anyone who asks questions.

WORSHIP GOD IN THE SPIRIT

"For we are the circumcision, which worship God in the spirit, and rejoice in Christ Jesus, and have no confidence in the flesh" (Philippians 3:3).

For it isn't the cutting of our bodies that makes us children of God; it is worshiping Him with our spirits and having faith in His work on the cross. This is the only true "circumcision." As christians we glory in what Christ Jesus has done for us and realize that we are helpless to save ourselves. "For in Christ Jesus neither circumcision availeth any thing, nor uncircumcision, but a new creature." (Galatians 6:15). As we become a new creature in Christ Jesus, we are brand new on the inside. We have no desire to do the things we once did. We begin a new life and that life is lived to please God and bless the people around us. God does it all! He puts the desire in our hearts. "For this is the covenant that I will make with the house of Israel after those days, saith the Lord; I will put my laws into their mind, and write them in their hearts: and I will be to them a God, and they shall be to me a people" (Hebrews 8:10).

HE SWARE BY HIMSELF

"For when God made promise to Abraham, because He could swear by no greater, He sware by Himself, Saying, Surely blessing I will bless thee, and multiplying I will multiply thee. And so, after he had patiently endured, he obtained the promise" (Hebrew 6:13–15).

God told Abraham that someday your descendants will be as numerous as the stars in the sky or the grains of the sand along the beach. They will defeat their enemies and take over their cities. He also said, because you have obeyed me, you and your descendants will be a blessing to all nations on earth. (Genesis 22:17). Long ago the scriptures said that God would accept the Gentiles because of their faith. That is why God told Abraham the good news that all the nations would be blessed because of him. So everyone who has the faith in God that Abraham had can receive these blessings. (Galatians 3:29). All of God's promises in the bible are for us. However, they are conditional. Many of them begin with "If". For instance: "If ye abide in me, and my words abide in you, ye shall ask what ye will, and it shall be done unto you" (John 15:7). We must abide in Him and His words abide in us before we can receive this promise. So let us wait patiently, and receive God's promises.

Chapter 11

LOVE GOD,
THE WRATH OF GOD,
MY GRACE IS SUFFICIENT,
PRESS TOWARD THE MARK,
ABIDE IN ME,
COMPLETE IN HIM.

LOVE GOD

"He that loveth father or mother more than me is not worthy of me: and he that loveth son or daughter more than me is not worthy of me. And he that taketh not his cross and followeth after me, is not worthy of me" (Matthew 10: 37, 38).

God commands us to love Him most of all. He must be first in our lives or not at all. "And thou shalt love the Lord thy God with all thy heart, and with all thy soul and with all thy mind, and with all thy strength; this is the first commandment. And the second is like, namely this, Thou shalt love thy neighbour as thyself. There is none other commandment greater than these" (Mark 12:30, 31). Understand that Jesus does want us to love others, but He must be first. Jesus must be first so that we may live obedient and holy lives. Everything falls in place When He is first, husbands are able to love their wives as Christ loved the church, wives are able to submit to their husbands, fathers are able to bring their children up in the nurture and admonition of the lord, children are able to obey their parents, and servants are able to be obedient to their masters. (Ephesians 5: 22, 25; 6:1, 4, 5). In order to love God first, we must take up our cross and follow Jesus. We take up our cross by following the example that He left for us. "And Jesus went about all the cities and villages teaching in their synagogues, and preaching the gospel of the kingdom, and healing every sickness and every disease among the people" (Matthew 9:35). You may be saying, "but I can't preach, or heal anyone." And this is true. We can do nothing without God. Neither could Jesus, He depended on God, the Father, for everything. "Believest thou that I am in the Father, and the Father in me? The words that I speak unto you I speak not of myself: but the Father that dwelleth in me, He doeth the works." (John 14:10). God use our bodies to do His work. We preach the word and the Holy Spirit convicts. We pray for the sick, but the Lord raises them up and forgives their sins. What a mighty God we serve!

THE WRATH OF GOD

"For the wrath of God is revealed from heaven against all ungodliness and unrighteousness of men, who hold the truth in unrighteousness; Because that which may be known of God is manifest in them, for God hath shewed it unto them" (Romans 1:18–20).

When we choose to disobey God we have decided to follow the deceiver (the devil). Because we have made the choice to choose the devil instead of God, He has no other choice but to allow the devil to do whatever he chooses to do in our lives. God displays His wrath toward the unrepentant sinner by withdrawing His protection from them and leaving them to contend with the forces of evil alone. "And the heathen shall know that the house of Israel went into captivity for their iniquity: because they trespassed against me therefore hid I my face from them and gave them into the hand of their enemies: so fell they all by the sword" (Ezekiel 39:23, 24). The Lord withheld His protection from Israel and they received recompense in direct proportion to their sins. The same principle applies to every individual who refuses to allow God to transform their character "Be sober, be vigilant; because your adversary the devil, as a roaring lion, walketh about, seeking whom he may devour" (I Peter 5:8).

MY GRACE IS SUFFICIENT

"And He said unto me, my grace is sufficient for thee: for my strength is made perfect in weakness. Most gladly therefore will I rather glory in my infirmities, that the power of Christ may rest upon me. Therefore I take pleasure in infirmities, in reproaches, in necessities, in persecution, in distresses for Christ's sake: for when I am weak, then am I strong" (II Corinthians 12: 9, 10).

Paul had a vision, he was caught up to heaven and heard unspeakable words, that he could not repeat. He said, "I would like to glory about it, but I won't. So that I would not be exalted, I was given a thorn in the flesh; a messenger of satan to buffet me that I may stay humble. I asked the Lord three times to deliver me from this, but He said, my grace is sufficient for thee" (II Corinthians 12:7). God's grace, His unmerited favor is enough to see us through any situation that comes into our lives. He further says, "For my strength is made perfect in weakness." So as we become weak He makes us strong. That seems like such an easy way to become strong, but we seem to have a problem with becoming weak. Is it because we want to be able to say, "I did it", those three words sound so good to our ears. "I am the vine, ye are the branches; He that abideth in me, and I in him, the same bringeth forth much fruit: for without me ye can do nothing" (John 15:5). We must always give God the glory for all the good we do, We must understand that we can do nothing without Him. He is the one who makes us strong. Although Paul's infirmity was not taken away, he still gave God the glory. We should glory also in our infirmities, so that more of God's power can rest upon us.

PRESS TOWARD THE MARK

"Brethren, I count not myself to have apprehended; but this one thing I do, forgetting those things which are behind, and reaching forth unto those things which are before, I press toward the mark for the prize of the high calling of God in Christ Jesus" (Philippians 3:13, 14).

Paul is saying, I am still not all that I should be, but I am causing all my energies to bear on one thing. Forgetting the past and looking forward to what lies ahead, I strain to reach the end, to receive the prize of God's high calling in Christ Jesus. Paul says, "forgetting those things which are behind." "The Past". We continue to live it over and over in our memory. But we can press toward the mark for the prize remembering this: "Therefore if any man be in Christ, he is a new creature: old things are passed away; behold, all things are become new" (II Corinthians 5:17). We are made new on the inside, squeaky clean, our thoughts, words and actions are not the same. We don't go to the same places. Our deepest desire is to please the Lord. Now we can move forward confidently with God because: "For whatsoever is born of God overcometh the world, even our faith" (I John 5:4). As we forget, reach, and press we will receive the "prize of the high calling of God in Christ Jesus.

ABIDE IN ME

"If ye abide in me, and my words abide in you, ye shall ask what ye will, and it shall be done unto you" (John 15:7).

Jesus says, "Ye shall ask what ye will and it shall be done unto you." Isn't that awesome! Then why are we denied so many requests? The clue here is: "If ye abide in me, and my words abide in you." This promise is upon conditions. Only if we abide in Him and His words abide in us will He be able to grant our requests. The more we love God; the more we are able to ask what we will without violating God's will. "If we abide in Him and His words abide in us" anything we ask is His desire for us. He will not force us to receive the goods things He has ready to give us; but we may have them only for the asking. Since God is so willing and ready to provide what we ask, we must have faith in His word. We ask timidly for some need to be met and then wait anxiously hoping that God will answer. Instead, we should trust God. "Therefore I say unto you, What things soever ye desire, when ye pray, believe that ye receive them, and ye shall have them" (Mark

11:24). Notice the scripture says, "Ye shall have them" meaning, some time in the future according to God's timing.

COMPLETE IN HIM

"For in Him dwelleth all the fullness of the God head bodily. And ye are complete in Him, which is the head of all principally and power" (Colossians 2:9, 10).

For in Christ there is all of God so we have everything when we have Christ. He is the highest ruler, with authority over every other power. Wrapped up in Jesus is everything we need. Human beings have four basic needs: food, shelter, clothing, and love, Jesus says, "Therefore take no thought, saying, What shall we eat? or, What shall we drink? or, Wherewithal shall we be clothed? (For all these things do the Gentiles seek) for your heavenly Father knoweth that ye have need of all these things. But seek ye first the kingdom of God; and His righteousness; and all these things shall be added unto you" (Matthew 6:31–33). When we realize that all of God's word is truth (John 17:17) and trust every single promise, then we will be complete in Him. Because we are complete in Christ, we don't have to live according to the world; trusting in man, instead of God. We never have to compromise because we know that all that we need comes from Jesus.

Chapter 12

ALL HAVE SINNED,
A PERFECT HEART,
NO COMMANDMENTS
GREATER THAN THESE,
OUR GREAT HIGH PRIEST.

ALL HAVE SINNED

"Wherefore, as by one man sin entered into the world and death by sin; and so death passed upon all men, for that all have sinned: For until the law sin was in the world: but sin is not imputed when there is no law" (Romans 5:12, 13).

When Adam sinned, sin entered the entire human race. Everyone began to grow old and die, for all sinned. Sin is the cause of it all! Sin caused all the evil in the world today. Sin damages our relationship with God, with each other and is the corruption of our entire being. It results with conflict and turmoil within us. Sin is not just what we do, but what we are. But thank God, we have the antidote for sin and it is the precious blood of Jesus. "Neither by the blood of goats and calves, but by His own blood He entered in once into the holy place, having obtained eternal redemption for us" (Hebrews 9:12). Jesus had to enter only once and that was sufficient to deliver us from the penalty of death. We no longer had to be slaves to sin. "But now being made free from sin, and become servants to God, ye have your fruit unto holiness, and the end everlasting life. For the wages of sin is death; but the gift of God is eternal life through Jesus Christ our Lord." (Romans 6:22–23). Jesus paid it all and all to Him we owe.

A PERFECT HEART

"For the eyes of the Lord run to and from throughout the whole earth, to shew Himself strong in the behalf of them whose heart is perfect toward Him. Herein thou hast done foolishly: therefore from henceforth thou shalt have wars" (II Chronicles 16:9).

When King Asa of Judah, was threatened by King Baasha of Israel, instead of trusting God; he took silver and gold from his palace and from the Lord's temple, and sent it to Demascus with a message to King Benhadad of Syria. The message said, I think we should sign a peace treaty just as our fathers did. Break your treaty with King Baasha and force him to leave my country. King Benhadad came to his rescue and saved him from the King of Israel. Afterwards, the prophet Hanani came to King Asa and told him, because you have put your trust in the King of Syria instead of the Lord your God, the King of Syria, has escaped from you. And you will never defeat them again. God is looking for a heart that is perfect toward Him. "Blessed is the man that walketh not in the counsel of the ungodly, nor standeth in the way of sinners, nor sitteth in the seat of the scornful. But his delight is in the law of the Lord; and in His law doth he meditate day and night" (Psalms 1:1, 2).

NO COMMANDMENTS GREATER THAN THESE

"And Jesus answered him. The first of all the commandments is , Hear, O Israel; The Lord our God is one Lord: And thou shalt love the Lord thy God with all thy heart, and with all thy soul, and with all thy mind, and with all thy strength: this is the first commandment. And the second is like, namely this, Thou shalt love thy neighbour as thyself. There is none other commandment greater than these" (Mark 12:29–31).

Until we love God supremely we cannot love our neighbour as ourselves. As we love our neighbor as ourselves all the law is fulfilled. "Owe no man any thing, but to love one another: for he that loveth another hath fulfilled the law" (Romans 13:8). When we love God supremely, we will have no other gods before Him, or make any graven image, or any likeness of any thing that is in heaven above, or use the name of the Lord thy God in vain, or forget to keep the sabbath day holy. If we love our neigbour as ourselves, we will honour our father and mother, we will not kill, will not commit adultery, will not steal, will not bear false witness,and will not covet anything of thy neighbour. As we go through life we should look for the best in others, and regard no one as hopeless. Love is a discipline as well as a feeling. Feelings are only a safeguard when in harmony with the word. Christ made the greatest decision of love in the garden when He said, "Nevertheless not as I will, but as thou wilt" (Matthew 26:39).

OUR GREAT HIGH PRIEST

"For we have not an high priest which cannot be touched with the feeling of our infirmities; but was in all points tempted like as we are, yet without sin. Let us therefore come boldly unto the throne of grace, that we may obtain mercy, and find grace to help in time of need." (Hebrews 4:15, 16).

Jesus, the Son of God, is our great High Priest who has gone to heaven to help us; therefore let us never stop trusting Him. He understands our weaknesses since He had the same temptations we do, but he never once gave way to them and sinned. We can do the same thing that He did, because He lived among the people and suffered and died for us. "For even hereunto were ye called: because Christ also suffered for us, leaving us an example, that ye should follow his steps: who did no sin, neither was guile found in His mouth: Who, when He was reviled, reviled not again; when He suffered, He threatened not; but committed Himself to Him that judgeth righteously." (I Peter 2:21–23). So let us come boldly unto the throne of unmerited favor to receive mercy in time of need. He will never turn away from us because we are His own. "Know therefore that the Lord thy God, He is God, the faithful God, which keepeth covenant and mercy with them that love him and keep His commandments to a thousand generations" (Deuteronomy 7:9).

Chapter 13

TRUST IN THE LORD,
THE LOVE OF MONEY,
GODLY SORROW WORKETH REPENTANCE,
SALVATION.

TRUST IN THE LORD

"Trust in the Lord with all thine heart; and lean not unto thine own understanding, In all thy ways acknowledge him, and He shall direct thy paths. Be not wise in thine own eyes; fear the Lord, and depart from evil." (Proverbs 3:5–7).

Don't ever trust yourself. In everything you do put God first, and He will direct you and crown your efforts with success. Don't be conceited, sure of your own wisdom. Instead, trust and reverence the Lord, and turn your back on evil. God has gone to great lengths to reveal His divine plan and purpose for our lives, but all too often we have chosen our own way. "Who hath saved us, and called us with an holy calling, not according to our works, but according to His own purpose and grace, which was given us in Christ Jesus before the world began" (II Timothy 1:9). God has chosen us for His holy work, not because we deserved it, but because that was His plan long before the world began, to show His love and kindness to us through Christ. When we trust in the Lord with all our heart, He will direct our path. When He directs our path we don't have to worry whether we are going in the right direction. As we trust in Him, His presence will guide, comfort, assure and empower us to follow His direction. As we trust Him we can say as David said: "Shew me thy ways, O Lord; teach me thy paths. Lead me in thy truth, and teach me: for thou art the God of my salvation; on thee do I wait all the day" (Psalms 25:4, 5).

THE LOVE OF MONEY

"For the love of money is the root of all evil: which while some coveted after, they have erred from the faith, and pierced themselves through with many sorrows." (I Timothy 6:10).

The love of money is the first step toward all kinds of sin. Some people have even turned away from God because of their love for it, How do we love money? First we must realize that money is a power with a life all by it self, It can be used to control, to buy prestige and honor, to enlist loyalty,and to corrupt people. We conquer money by placing it under the blood of the lamb. "And almost all things are by the law purged with blood; and without shedding of blood is no remission" (Hebrews 9:22). When we repent of the love of money, we allow God to determine our economic decisions. When God determines our economic decision, we only buy things, when God has given us permission; not because we have the money to buy them, or because we want them. We can go to God without money when needs and desires arise in our lives and He will provide. As we keep the money flowing through our hands by meeting the needs of others we dethrone the power of money by giving it away. By giving we are never without. "Give, and it shall be given unto you; good measure, pressed down, and shaken together, and running over, shall men give into your bosom, for with the same measure that ye mete withal it shall be measured to you again" (Luke 6:38). When we give, we get gifts, that return to us in full and overflowing measures.

GODLY SORROW WORKETH REPENTANCE

"Now I rejoice, not that ye were made sorry, but that ye sorrowed to repentance: for ye were made sorry after a godly manner, that ye might receive damage by us in nothing. For godly sorrow worketh repentance to salvation not to be repented of: but the sorrow of the world worketh death" (II Corinthians 7:9, 10).

Godly sorrow comes from God, when we have this sorrow we are truly sorrowful and turn from the sin we have committed. But the sorrow of the world means being sorry that we got caught. For example: A person that robs a bank and is caught is sorry not for what he did, but that he knows he is going to be punished. If he has a chance he will do it again, but perhaps in a different way. Whether we have godly sorrow, or sorrow that we got caught, there are consequences that we must suffer. When David had Uriah, the Hittite, killed in battle and Nathan came and told him what God said, he had godly sorrow and repented. "And David said unto Nathan, I have sinned against the Lord, and Nathan said unto David, The Lord also hath put away thy sin; thou shalt not die. Now therefore the sword shall never depart from thine house; because thou hast despised me, and hast taken the wife of Uriah the Hittite to be thy wife. Thus saith the Lord, Behold, I will raise up evil against thee out of thine own house, and I will take thy wives before thine eyes, and give them unto thy neighbour, and he shall lie with thy wives in the sight of this sun" (II Samuel 12:10, 11). David was forgiven but he suffered terrible consequences from his own family because of his sins.

SALVATION

"Therefore by the deeds of the law there shall no flesh be justified in His sight: for by the law is knowledge of sin. For all have sinned, and come short of the glory of God; Being justified freely by His grace through the redemption that is in Christ Jesus" (Romans 3:20, 23, 24).

Salvation consists of three parts, Justification, sanctification and glorification. Justification removes all the sins of the past, and we are cleansed from all unrighteousness. This miracle takes place instantly. I am delivered from the penalty of sin on the spot. It is called the new birth; there is no past, I am a new creature. "Therefore if any man be in Christ, he is a new creature: old things are passed away; behold all things are become new" (II Corinthians 5:17). Sanctification is right living or holiness. Growth is another name for sanctification. To be born is a wonderful miracle, but it is not enough. We must grow. It is a great tragedy when a baby is born but never grows. It is a great spiritual tragedy when a person experiences the new birth but never grows. Sanctification is God power saving us from sin's power, "As newborn babes, desire the sincere milk of the word, that ye may grow thereby" (I Peter 2:2). When we obey the word of God, we will grow into strong christians. We obtain Glorification at Jesus return. "Behold, I shew you a mystery; We shall not all sleep, but we shall all be changed, In a moment, in the twinkling of an eye, at the last trump: for the trumpet shall sound, and the dead shall be raised incorruptible, and we shall be changed. For this corruptible must put on incorruption, and this mortal must put on immortality. So when this corruptible shall have put on incorruption, and this mortal shall have put on immortality, then shall be brought to pass the saying that is written, Death is swallowed up in victory. O death, where is thy sting: O grave, where is thy victory? The sting of death is sin and the strength of sin is the law: But thanks be to God, which giveth us the victory through our Lord Jesus Christ" (I Corinthians 15:51–57).

Chapter 14

GOD'S OWN PURPOSE,
FULLNESS OF JOY,
SOW THY SEED,
UNMERITED FAVOR.

GOD'S OWN PURPOSE

"Who hath saved us, and called us with an holy calling, not according to our works, but according to His own purpose and grace, which was given us in Christ Jesus before the world began" (II Timothy 1:9).

Purpose is the key to fulfillment, God is a God of purpose. Everything in life has a purpose, but not every purpose is known. We don't know our true purpose; that is why we must ask our Father because He knows all things. "If any of you lack wisdom, let him ask of God, that giveth to all men liberally, and upbraideth not; and it shall be given him. But let him ask in faith, nothing wavering. For he that wavereth is like a wave of the sea driven with the wind and tossed. For let not that man think that he shall receive any thing of the Lord" (James 1:5–7). If we want to know what God wants us to do, we must ask Him, and He will gladly tell us, for He is always ready to give a bountiful supply of wisdom to all that ask Him. When God reveal to us His purpose for our lives He will also give us the directions and power to fulfill our purpose. "And thine ears shall hear a word behind thee, saying, This is the way, walk ye in it, when ye turn to the right hand, and when ye turn to the left" (Isaiah 30:21). God will always guide us but we must make the choice to follow Him.

FULLNESS OF JOY

"Thou wilt shew me the path of life: in thy presence is fulness of joy; at thy right hand there are pleasures for evermore" (Psalms 16:11).

Joy can only come from being in the presence of the Lord. So how do we come into His presence? First we must recieve the new birth. When Nicodemus came to Jesus he wanted to be in God's presence. What did Jesus tell him? "Verily, verily, I say unto thee, Except a man be born again, He cannot see the kingdom of God" (John 3:3). Second, we must desire to follow Him. "And He said to them all, If any man will come after me, let him deny himself, and take up his cross daily, and follow me" (Luke 9:23). We must put aside our own desires and conveniences and follow His example. Third, we must have a burden to win lost people to Christ. After His resurrection He gave His disciples the great commission. "And Jesus came and spake unto them, saying, All power is given unto me in heaven and in earth. Go ye therefore, and teach all nations, baptizing them in the name of the Father, and of the Son, and of the Holy Ghost: Teaching them to observe all things whatsoever I have commanded you: and, lo, I am with you always, even unto the end of the world" (Matthew 28:19, 20). If we have received the new birth, then we are His disciples also. We should be making disciples every where we go, teaching these new disciples to obey all the commandments and believing that Jesus is with us always, even to the end of the world. Certainly we are in His presence as we accept His payment for our sins, following His example daily, and witnessing to lost people.

SOW THY SEED

"He that observeth the wind shall not sow; and he that regardeth the clouds shall not reap. As thou knowest not what is the way of the spirit, nor how the bones do grow in the womb of her that is with child: even so thou knowest not the works of God who maketh all. In the morning sow thy seed, and in the evening withold not thine hand: for thou knowest not whether they both shall be alike good" (Ecclesiastes 11:4–6).

If we wait for perfect conditions or weather we will never plant seeds. We will never harvest a crop or succeed in life. We don't know the way of the spirit or how a baby forms in the womb. We don't understand the ways of God. "For my thouthts are not your thoughts, neither are your ways my ways, saith the Lord. For as the heavens are higher than the earth, so are my ways higher than your thoughts" (Isaiah 55:8, 9). So we must continue sowing seeds because we don't know which one will grow. But when we trust God in faith we receive His best. "And we know that all things work together for good to them that love God, to them who are the called according to His purpose" (Romans 8:28). As we fit into His plan, all things will work together for our good. As we continue to sow our seeds of love, forgiveness, money, and peace they will all come back to us. "Cast thy bread upon the waters: for thou shalt find it after many days" (Ecclesiastes 11:1). So don't get tired of doing what is right, for after a while, we will receive a harvest of blessing, if we don't get discouraged and give up.

UNMERITED FAVOR

"For I am the least of the apostles, that am not meet to be called an apostle, because I persecuted the church of God. But by the grace of God I am what I am: and His grace which was bestowed upon me was not in vain; but I laboured more abundantly than they all: yet not I, but the grace of God which was with me" (I Corinthians 15:9, 10).

Paul is saying whatever I am now it is all because God poured out such kindnes and grace upon me and not without results: for I have worked harder than all the other apostles, but I wasn't doing it, but God working in me, to bless me. Paul confesses his sin, and we must also confess because none of us have been good. We have not all committed the same sins, but all trangressions are sin. Grace is unmerited favor of God. We don't deserve it, but because God is love, He bestows grace upon us. If you are satisfied where you are today, be grateful; if not, hang in there, there is hope for you. In our scripture Paul is speaking of his life before and after he became a christian. On the Damacus Road, Paul had an encounter with Jesus and he was never the same again. A great light shined around him and he fell to the ground. He heard a voice saying, "Saul, Saul, why persecutest thou me?" (Acts 9:4). When Paul found out that it was Jesus he said, "Lord what will thou have me to do? (Acts 9:6). God will use us the same way that he used Paul. We only have to be willing to do what He says. "Then Peter opened his mouth, and said, of a truth I perceive that God is no respecter of persons; But in every nation he that feareth Him, and worketh righterosness, is accepted with Him" (Acts 10:34, 35). Are we laboring for the cause of Christ, since God delivered us from the hands of the devil?

Chapter 15

WHATSOEVER HE DOETH SHALL PROSPER, ATTEND TO MY WORDS, BLESSED WITH ALL SPIRITUAL BLESSINGS, GREAT PEACE, POVERTY AND SHAME, DAVID'S SONG OF PRAISE.

WHATSOEVER HE DOETH SHALL PROSPER

"Blessed is the man that walketh not in the counsel of the ungodly, nor standeth in the way of sinners, nor sitteth in the seat of the scornful. But his delight is in the law of the Lord; and in His law doth he meditate day and night. And he shall be like a tree planted by the rivers of water, that bringeth forth his fruit in his season; his leaf also shall not wither; and whatsoever he doeth shall prosper" (Psalms 1:1, 2, 3).

The definition of Blessed is: holy; sacred, full of bliss; fortunate. Blessed and God go together like faith and works they cannot be separated. Although God bless us, we are not always happy; our reaction to God's blessings determines whether we are happy or not. If you separate God from blessed, then you have the world happiness; a happiness that does not last, it is here today and gone tomorrow, It depends upon our circumstances. However, we can be blessed all the time in Jesus, no matter what is going on in our lives. When we delight in doing God's law, we will not listen to the counsel of the ungodly, or constantly be in the company of sinners, who don't believe any of God's word. We will think of ways to follow Him more closely and as we do, whatsoever we do will prosper. It will prosper because what ever we do will be pleasing to God. "If ye abide in me, and my words abide in you, ye shall ask what ye will, and it shall be done unto you. I am the vine, ye are the branches; He that abideth in me, and I in him, the same bringeth forth much fruit; for without me ye can do nothing" (John 15:5). So as we delight in His law and mediate upon his law day and night every victory will be won, every temptation will be resisted, every sin forgiven and every blessing enjoyed.

ATTEND TO MY WORDS

"My son, attend to my words; incline thine ear unto my sayings. Let them not depart from thine eyes; keep them in the midst of thine heart. For they are life unto those that find them, and health to all thy flesh." (Proverbs 4:20–22).

Solomon says, if you want to have life (eternal) and not death, health and not sickness, then listen carefully to what I have to say. Keep God's words in your heart. Let them penetrate, because they will not only give you eternal life, but an abundant life here on earth. These words will guard your affection, will influence every choice you make, will keep corrupt talk from your lips, keep your feet in the right path and keep your eyes from lust. David said, "I will set no wicked thing before mine eyes: I hate the work of them that turn aside; it shall not cleave to me" (Psalms 101:3). He says I will not look at vulgar things, or have anything to do with crooked deals. God's words are also health to our bodies. If we constantly study God's word, we will saturate ourselves with His word and there will be no room for sickness; sickness can not thrive in a mind full of the word. "It shall be health to thy navel and marrow to thy bones" (Proverbs 3:8). The word of God will bring healing, to your mind and body and nourishment to your bones.

BLESSED WITH ALL SPIRITUAL BLESSINGS

"Blessed be the God and Father of our Lord Jesus Christ, who hath blessed us with all spiritual blessings in heavenly places in Christ. According as He hath chosen us in Him before the foundation of the world, that we should be holy and without blame before Him in love." (Ephesians 1:3, 4).

Long ago, even before He made the world, God chose us to be His very own, through what Christ would do for us; He decided then to make us holy in His eyes, without a single fault, covered with His love. When we are blessed with spiritual blessings, that is all that we need, because All material blessings flow from the spiritual realm. Everything we will ever need is already in the spiritual realm; and as we pray and trust God, He will manifest it to us. We can't see them with the natural eye, but God can reveal them to us when He chooses to. Abraham sent Hagar and Ishmael away from their home with him; and when her water bottle was empty, and she began to think about the death of her son, she began to cry. "And God opened her eyes, and she saw a well of water; and she went, and filled the bottle with water, and gave the lad drink" (Genesis 21:19). Her natural eyes were opened all the time, but God opened her spiritual eyes so that she could see the well of water. Nothing catches God by surprise, He knew before the foundation of the world that man would sin, therefore, He made provisions for us to be holy and without blame before Him in love. He made this possible by sending His only begotten Son to die for us. "Wherefore when He cometh into the world, He saith, sacrifice and offering thou wouldest not, but a body hast thou prepared me." (Hebrews 10:5). Jesus said the sacrifice of the blood of bulls and goats can not satisfy, so you have made me a body that I might be the perfect sacrifice for sin.

GREAT PEACE

"Great peace have they which love thy law and nothing shall offend them" (Psalms 119:165).

When we love the law we will obey it and will have peace. If we have this peace it will hardly even notice when others mistreat us. When we are blessed with the peace of God, we rely on the love and grace of God to work out every situation, that arise in our lives. With God's peace there will be no dread of tomorrow. The word peace carries with it the idea of completeness, good welfare and health. The word peace incorporates every aspect of life including the physical, mental, spiritual, whether individually, collectively and nationally. Jesus is the prince of peace, in Him through faith and obedience to both moral and physical laws we can find peace. "My son, forget not my law; but let thine heart keep my commandments: For length of days and long life, and peace shall they add to thee" (Proverbs 3:1–2). Jesus is the peace giver. The peace He gives last forever. God's peace and worldy peace are different. "Peace I leave with you, my peace I give unto you: not as the world giveth, give I unto you, let not your heart be troubled, neither let it be afraid" (John 14:27).

POVERTY AND SHAME

"Poverty and shame shall be to him that refuseth instruction: but he that regardeth reproof shall be honoured" (Proverbs 13:18).

When we do not accept good instructions and decide to experience everything, because we believe things will work out differently for us, we find ourselves in poverty and shame. The Prodigal Son is a very good example. The son asked his father for his share of the estate and the father gave it to him. He went out and wasted all his money in parties and women. When all his money was gone, there was a great famine in the land, and he began to starve. He was hired to feed the pigs and he became so hungry, that the food he fed the pigs appealed to him, but no one gave him anything. Then he came to his senses, he said to himself, at home even the hired servants have plenty of food to spare, and I am here dying of hunger! I will go home to my father. "And the son said unto him, Father, I have sinned against heaven, and in thy sight, and am no more worthy to be called thy son. But the father said to his servants, Bring forth the best robe, and put it on him; and put a ring on his hand, and shoes on his feet: And bring hither the fatted calf, and kill it; and let us eat, and be merry: For this my son was dead, and is alive again; he was lost, and is found. And they began to be merry"(Luke 11:21–24). This son did not understand the value of money and suffered the consequences of poverty and shame. However, he had a loving father who forgave him and restored their relationship. And we also have a loving heavenly father who will always forgive us when we come to our senses and repent. "If we confess our sin, he is faithful and just to forgive us our sins, and to cleanse us from all unrighteousness" (I John 1:9).

DAVID'S SONG OF PRAISE

"And he said, The Lord is my rock, and my fortress, and my deliverer; The God of my rock; in him will I trust: he is my shield and the horn of my salvation, my high tower, and my refuge, my saviour; thou savest me from violence. I will call on the Lord, who is worthy to be praised: so shall I be saved from mine enemies" (II Samuel 22:2–4).

David sang to the Lord the words of this song, when the Lord delivered him from the hand of all his enemies and from the hand of Saul. He sang to God a song of praise, and it wasn't a short praise, it was twenty-nine verses long. His song encompassed the greatness, the mercifulness and the perfectness of God. He let God know, that he knew, He was the one that brought him out triumphantly, over his enemies. "He saved me from powerful enemies, From those who hated me and from those who were too strong for me. They came upon me in the day of my calamity, But the Lord was my salvation. He set me free and rescued me, For I was His delight. The Lord rewarded me for my goodness, For my hands were clean; And I have not departed from my God. I knew His laws, And I obeyed in obedience and kept myself from sin. You are merciful to the merciful; You show your perfection to the blameless" (II Samuel 22:18–26).

Chapter 16

PRAYER OF THE RIGHTEOUS AVAILETH, CONFESS AND FORSAKE.

PRAYER OF THE RIGHTEOUS AVAILETH

"Confess your faults one to another, and pray one for another, that ye may be healed. The effectual fervent prayer of a righteous man availeth much. Elias was a man subject to like passions as we are, and he prayed earnestly that it might not rain: and it rained not on the earth by the space of three years and six months. And he prayed again, and the heaven gave rain, and the earth brought forth her fruit" (James 5:16–18).

The verse says, confess your faults, not your sins. No where in the bible are we told to confess our sins one to another. Our sins are to be confessed to God, because He is the only one that can forgive sin. "If we confess our sin He is faithful and just to forgive us our sins, and to cleanse us for all unrighteousness" (I John 1:9). Isn't it wonderful that we can keep a right relationship with God by coming to Him when we sin asking for forgiveness for our sins, As we confess our faults one to another and the righteous man prays, the effectual fervent prayer, we can be healed. We can be delivered from what caused us not to be able to live that purposeful life, that God desires for us. There are times when we are overwhelmed and don't feel like praying, but that is the time we need to pray the most. Many times we fail to pray because the devil tells us we are not righteous and God will not hear us. "For what saith the scripture? Abraham believed God, and it was counted unto him for righteousness" (Romans 4:3). When we trust Jesus as our Lord and saviour He gives us His righteousness and God sees us as sinless. Elias was a human being just like us and he prayed earnestly that it might not rain and it didn't rain for three and one-half years.

Because Elias prayers were answered, God will answer our earnest prayers also. "Then Peter opened his mouth, and said, of a truth I perceive that God is no respecter of person: But in every nation he that feareth Him,and worketh righteousness, is accepted with Him " (Acts 10:34, 35).

CONFESS AND FORSAKE

"He that covers his sins shall not prosper; but whoso confesseth and forsaketh them shall have mercy" (Proverbs 28:13).

Whatever is hidden and concealed will be brought out into the open. However, in order to prosper we must not only confess our sin, but we must turn from them. Zacchaeus is a good example of a person that was willing to turn from his sin. "And Zacchaeus stood, and said unto the Lord; Behold, Lord, the half of my goods I give to the poor; and if I have taken any thing from any man by false accusation, I restore him fourfold. And Jesus said unto him, This day is salvation come to this house, forsomuch as he also is a son of Abraham. For the Son of man is come to seek and to save that which was lost" (Luke 19:8–10). Because Zacchaeus was willing, to make right what he had done, God had mercy on him and saved him. Confession brings possession. As we confess God's word over our lives, we will reap all the benefits of the word. "So shall my word be that goeth forth out of my mouth: it shall not return unto me void, but it shall accomplish that which I please, and it shall prosper in the thing whereto I sent it" (Isaiah 55:11). God's word always prospers where He sends it.

Chapter 17

MY NOURISHMENT IS TO DO HIS WILL, BLESSED IS HE, LABOR NOT TO BE RICH, INSPIRATION OF GOD, MOLD THE CHILD, ENDURE TEMPTATION, THOUGHTS OF PEACE, JESUS IS THE VINE.

MY NOURISHMENT IS TO DO HIS WILL

"Jesus saith, unto them, My meat is to do the will of Him that sent me, and to finish His work" (John 4:34).

Jesus disciples had gone into the city to buy food. When they returned with the food they urged Jesus to eat, but He said, I have food to eat that you don't know about. The disciples asked did someone bring you food? Jesus said, My food is to do the will of Him that sent me. Jesus had a purpose and that purpose consumed His entire being so much that He forgot about food. Have you ever done something, that you liked so well, that you have forgotten completely about lunch? Then you can understand how Jesus felt. The work that so consumed Jesus was lost people. "Say not ye, There are yet four months and then cometh the harvest? Behold, I say unto you, lift up your eyes, and look on the fields; for they are white already to harvest" (John 4:35). Jesus was saying, do you think, the work of the harvest won't begin until four more months? Look around you many souls are ready for reaping. We should have a burden, on our hearts to bring Lost people into the kingdom of God, that should be our greatest desire, as it was for Jesus. Jesus told his disciple, "Go ye into all the world, and preach the gospel to every creature. He that believeth and is baptized shall be saved; but he that believeth not shall be damned" (Mark 16:15, 16). If you have received Jesus as your Lord and saviour then you are His disciple and you should be telling people about the good news. "The Good News Is," Jesus loves you and came to save you. "The thief cometh not, but for to steal, and to kill, and to destroy: I am come that they might have life, and that they might have it more abundantly" (John 10:10).

BLESSED IS HE

"Then Jesus answering said unto them, Go your way, and tell John what things ye have seen and heard; how that the blind see, the lame walk, the lepers are cleansed, the deaf hear, the dead are raised, to the poor the gospel is preached. And blessed is he, whosoever shall not be offended in me" (Luke 7:22, 23).

John sent his disciples to ask Jesus, "Art thou He that should come? Or look we for another? I believe John's faith was beginning to waiver, because he had been thrown in prison. We might be asking ourselves how could John ask Jesus that question? He was the one that said, "Behold the Lamb of God which taketh away the sins of the world" (John 1:29). We really don't know what John's reason was, for sending the disciples to Jesus, with this question. It might have been that his disciples needed assurance, that Jesus was the Messiah, or that John had some misgiving, of his own about the Messianic kingdom being ushered in as he thought, or perhaps he thought he had been forgotten, while others were helped. In Jesus answer, he let John and his disciples know why He came. He not only came to save us from our sins, but to heal us and to prosper us. Jesus also said, "Blessed is he, whoever shall not be offended in me" (Matthew 7:23). Jesus wants us to trust Him, even when He does things that we don't understand.

LABOR NOT TO BE RICH

"Labour not to be rich; cease from thine own wisdom. Wilt thou set thine eyes upon that which is not?" (Proverbs 23:4).

"But they that will be rich fall into temptation and a snare, and into many foolish and hurtful lusts, which drown men in destruction and perdition" (I Timothy 6:9). People who long to be rich, began to do all kinds of wrong things to get money, things that hurt, make them evil-minded, and they finally lose their souls. We are not supposed to work to become rich, but to take care of our needs. We work so hard for things, when all we need to do is put God first. "But seek ye first the kingdom of God, and His righteousness; and all these things shall be added unto you" (Matthew 6:33). We put the cart before the horse. We use our own wisdom and believe our way is better than God's way. The scripture says, "And all these things shall be added unto you" Things such as: joy, peace, health, prosperity and love. In seeking God's kingdom first, you not only receive the abundant life here on earth, but eternal life as well. "And there shall be no night there; and they need no candle, neither light of the sun; for the Lord God giveth them light: and they shall reign for ever and ever" (Revelation 22:5).

INSPIRATION OF GOD

"All scripture is given by inspiration of God, and is profitable for doctrine, for reproof, for correction, for instruction in righteousness. That the man of God may be perfect, throughly furnished unto all good works" (II Timothy 3:16, 17).

The whole bible was given to us from God, and is useful to teach us what is true and to help us realize, what is wrong in our lives. It's God's way of making us well prepared at every point. Fully equipped to do good to everyone. Since we have been given this book of life, we must use it in the proper way to get the full understanding. We must study the bible with the help of the Holy Spirit. As we open our bible we must first pray and ask the Holy Spirit, to reveal the interpretation of the scripture as we study. However, we must understand that we can't choose one scripture and determine the meaning of a particular verse. We must study at least four or five scriptures, or more on that particular subject, to draw the right conclusion. "Study to shew thyself approved unto God, a workman that needeth not to be ashamed, rightly dividing the word of truth" (II Timothy 2:15).

MOLD THE CHILD

"Train up a child in the way he should go: and when he is old, he will not depart from it" (Proverbs 22:6).

All children have different personalities and must be trained in a way that best fits his or her needs. Children physical and emotional needs must be met. Food, shelter, clothing and unconditional love, in order to grow up emotional healthy. And they must receive spiritual training to live a successful life to get from earth to heaven. The great error that parents make is not portraying a personal loving relationship with God in their home. Children won't love God unless they see their parents in a loving releationship with Him. This training should also consist of chasteneth in a form that works. "He that spareth his rod hateth his son: but he that loveth him chasteneth him betimes" (Proverbs 13:24). Being consistent is the key. There is a very special message for fathers in (Ephesians 6:4), "And, ye fathers, provoke not your children to wrath: but bring them up in the nurture and admonition of the Lord". (Colossians 3:21), tells us: "Fathers, provoke not your children to anger lest they be discouraged". This scripture says, fathers don't keep on scolding and nagging your children, making them angry and resentful. Rather, bring them up with loving discipline, and godly advice. Training children is a great responsibility and it should not be taken lightly. When we train our children as God has admonished us, we can give them back to God with a clear conscious knowing that we have done accordingly to "Thus says the Lord."

ENDURE TEMPTATION

"Blessed is the man that endureth temptation for when he is tried, he shall receive the crown of life, which the Lord has promised to them that love Him" Let no man say when he is tempted, I am tempted of God: for God cannot be tempted with evil, neither tempteth He any man: But every man is tempted,

when he is drawn away of his own lust and enticed" (James 1:12, 13, 14).

Blessed is the man that does not give in and do wrong when he is tempted, for afterwards he will receive the crown of life, that God has promised to those that love Him. How do we know that we love him? We can't trust our feelings because they change from moment to moment. We love Him when we keep His commandments. "He that hath my commandments, and keepeth them, he it is that loveth me: and he that loveth me shall be loved of my Father, and I will love him. And manifest myself to him" (John 14:21). Since we know that temptation, is the pull of man's own evil thoughts and desires, we must allow our minds to be changed. "And be not conformed to this world: but be ye transformed by the renewing of your mind, that ye may prove what is that good, and acceptable and perfect, will of God" (Romans 12:2). Don't conform be transformed. How do we renew our minds? By putting in the word of God, we continually saturate our being with God's word, and our mind will become new, with the thoughts of God. Then we will know what is good, acceptable, and perfect.

THOUGHTS OF PEACE

"For I know the thoughts I think toward you, saith the Lord, thoughts of peace, and not of evil, to give you an expected end. Then shall ye call upon me, and ye shall go and pray unto me, and I will hearken unto you. And ye shall seek me, and find me, when ye shall search for me with all your heart" (Jeremiah 29:11–13).

Jerusalem, the capital city, was completely destroyed, and many of the people of Judah and Jerusalem were led away as prisoners to Babylonia. King Nebuchadnezzar made Gedaliah, ruler over those left in Judah. This scripture tells us that the Lord had not forgotten them. He told them that He had good plans for them, a future and a hope. He also said, when you pray and search for me, with all your heart you will find me. God allowed the people to be carried away as prisoners, because they had been unfaithful to Him. After sending prophet after prophet to warn them, they would not listen to Him. This scripture is for us today, We have become unfaithful to Him as Judah and Jerusalem had. "For men shall be lovers of their own selves, covetous, boaters, proud, blasphemers, disobedient to parents, unthankful, unholy, Without natural affection, trucebreakers, false accusers, incontinent, fierce, despisers of those that are good, Traitors, heady, highminded, lovers of pleasures more than lovers of God" (II Timothy 3:2–4). However, God still has good thouthts towards us, and want to give us a happy end. God is our "Sar-Shalom" The prince of peace and through obedience to His laws, both moral and physical we will find wholeness, completeness, and well being in our lives.

JESUS IS THE VINE

"I am the vine, ye are the branches: He that abideth in me, and I in him, the same bringeth forth much fruit: for without me ye can do nothing" (John 15:5).

Jesus is the vine and if we abide in Him we can get the nourishment to bring forth much fruit. Never ever think that you can do anything good without Him. How do we abide in Him? First of all we must love! "Jesus said unto him, Thou shalt love the Lord thy God with all thy heart, and with all thy soul, and with all thy mind. This is the first and great commandment. And the second is like unto it, Thou shalt love thy neighbour as thyself. On these two commandments hang all the law and the prophets" (Matthew 22:37–39). As we love we can abide in Him. This fruit is seen in soul winning. "I have planted, Apollos watered; but God gave the increase. So then neither is he that planteth any thing, neither he that watereth; but God that giveth the increase" (I Corinthians 3:6, 7). We must ask God each day to bring someone across our path, that we may tell about the love of Jesus. As we plant, someone else will water and God will give the increase.

Chapter 18

NOAH FOUND GRACE, GOD WORKETH IN YOU, FORGIVE AND BE FREE.

NOAH FOUND GRACE

"And it repented the Lord that He had made man on the earth, and it grieved Him at His heart. And the Lord said, I will destroy man whom I have created from the face of the earth, both man, and beast, and creeping thing, and the fowls of the air, for it repenteth me that I have made them. But Noah found grace in the eyes of the Lord" (Genesis 6:6–8).

When the Lord saw the extent of human wickedness, and that the direction of men's lives was only towards evil, He was sorry He had made man. It grieved His heart and He decided to destroy man, beast, creepings things and the fowls of the air. "But Noah found grace in the eyes of the Lord." Noah was a just man and perfect in his generation and Noah walked with God. The Lord told Noah to make an ark and He was going to establish a covenant with him to save he and his family. "Of every clean beast thou shalt take to thee by seven, the male and his female: and of beasts that are not clean by two, the male and his female. Of fowls also of the air by sevens, the male and the female; to keep seed alive upon the face of all the earth" (Genesis 7:2, 3). It took Noah one hundred and twenty years to build the ark. The ark had three stories. "And they that went in, went in male and female of all flesh, as God had commanded him : and the Lord shut him in. And every living substance was destroyed which was upon the face of the ground, both man, and cattle, and the creeping things, and the fowl of the heaven, and they were destroyed from the earth and Noah only remained alive, and they that were with him in the ark. And the waters prevailed upon the earth an hundred and fifty days" (Genesis 7:16, 23). And because of God's grace Noah and his family were saved and we are the generations of Noah, a just and perfect man, because he obeyed God.

GOD WORKETH IN YOU

"For it is God which worketh in you both to will and do of His good pleasure" (Philippians 2:13).

God will equip us with all we need for doing His will, He will produce in us, through the power of Christ, all that is pleasing to Him. We can do nothing on our own because Jesus said: "Believest thou not that I am in the Father, and the Father in me? The words that I speak unto you I speak not of myself: but the Father that dwelleth in me, He doeth the works" (John 14:10). God worked His work in Jesus because Jesus relied on Him for everything. God worked through Jesus and God allows Jesus, to work through us to do His good pleasure. When we begin to realize, that we are not able to do anything, without God, then and only then will we be able to live a victorious christian life.

FORGIVE AND BE FREE

"Then came Peter to Him, and said Lord, how oft shall my brother sin against me, and I forgive him? Till seven times? Jesus saith unto him, I say not unto thee, until seven times: but, until seventy times seven" (Matthew 18:21, 22).

Three of the hardest things to do is: to ask for forgiviness, to forgive someone, and to forgive ourselves. However, we must understand that Jesus had His reasons for telling us to forgive. If we don't forgive others God won't forgive us. (Matthew 6:15). Our gifts will not be accepted if our brother hath ought against us. (Matthew 5:23, 24). And unforgiviness causes stress, which leads to all kinds of illness. It dosen't make any difference whether I offend or the other person, we must make it right. When we are angry with a person, it gives satan a foothold. "Be ye angry, and sin not: let not the sun go down upon your wrath: Neither give place to the devil" (Ephesians 4:26, 27). When we nurse our anger we allow satan to put negative thoughts into our mind and if we are not careful, we will follow through on them. We must pray, and ask God to forgive us, and then, He blesses us in such an awesome way! He set us free, free to love, to forgive and accept people just where they are. If there is unforgiviness in your heart, make it right today.

Chapter 19

THE FATHER DWELLETH IN ME, WAIT ON THE LORD

THE FATHER DWELLETH IN ME

"Believest thou not that I am in the Father, and the Father in me? The words that I speak unto you I speak not of myself: but the Father that dwelleth in me, He doeth the works" (John 14:10).

Phillip asked Jesus the question, "Lord shew us the Father, and it sufficeth us." Jesus said to him, all this time that I have been with you and you have not known me? Jesus went on to say he that hath seen me has seen the Father. Then he tells Phillip, "But the Father that dwelleth in me, He doeth the works. All of Jesus power came from God. He did nothing without God's help. That was His example for us, so that we would rely on God's help, because without Him we can do nothing. We are trying to do everything by ourselves and that is why the devil is destroying us. "I can do all things through Christ who strengtheneth me" (Philippians 4:13). We can do all things that God asks us to do, with the help of Christ who gives us the strength and power. We must realize, that Jesus didn't do any miraculous things, without God working them through Him. Knowing this should give us confidence, that if God worked through Jesus, He will work through us also. When Jesus needed to make decisions, He prayed to the Father. "And it came to pass in those days, that He went out into a mountain to pray, and continued all night in prayer to God. And when it was day, He called unto Him His disciples: and of them He chose twelve, whom also he named apostles" (Luke 6:12, 13). In such a great decision He needed the Fathers help.

WAIT ON THE LORD

"Wait on the Lord: be of good courage, and He shall strength-en thine heart: wait I say, on the Lord" (Psalms 27:14).

Don't be impatient. The Lord will come and save you. Be brave, stouthearted and courageous. The Lord will come when the time is right. "But when the fulness of the time was come, God sent forth His Son, made of a woman, made under the law" (Galatians 4:4.) All of the men that were used of God had to wait. Moses tended sheep for forty years and became the deliverer for the Israelites (Exodus 3). Abraham waited for 25 years for the promise child and became the Father of many nations (Genesis 21). Joseph waited in prison for two years and was made ruler over all the land of Egypt (Genesis 41:43). God's timing is always right. That is why we should wait on the Lord. "My soul, wait thou only upon God; for my expectation is from Him" (Psalms 62:5). The strengthening of our heart is when God give us the strength to obey His word. "Then Peter and the other apostles answered and said, We ought to obey God rather than men. (Acts 5:29).

Chapter 20

WILL YOU BE ABLE TO STAND, THE WORD DIVIDES SOUL AND SPIRIT, HE GAVE THEM THEIR REQUEST.

WILL YOU BE ABLE TO STAND

"If thou hast run with the footmen, and they have wearied thee, then how canst thou contend with horses? And if in the land of peace, wherein thou trustedst, they wearied thee, then how wilt thou do in the swelling of Jordan?" (Jeremiah 12:5).

The Lord tells Jeremiah, if the people have raced with men on foot and they have worn you out, how can they compete with horses? If the army stumble in safe country how will they manage in the thickets by the Jordan? This was a physical battle, but ours is a spiritual battle. I ask the question if we are falling away from God, when we are free to worship Him, what will we do when persecution begin? The enemy is getting bolder every day, what we are experiencing now is just the tip of the iceberg. We are living in the time of the end now, but when the end of time is upon us,will we be able to stand against the evil one? We must strengthen ourselves in the word of God, in the time of peace. "For in those days shall be affliction, such as was not from the beginning of the creation which God created unto this time, neither shall be. And except that the Lord has shortened those days, no flesh should be saved: but for the elect's sake, whom He hath chosen, He hath shortened the days. And then if any man shall say to you, lo, here is Christ; or lo, He is there; believe him not: For false Christs and false prophets shall rise, and shall shew signs and wonders, to seduce, if it were possible, even the elect" (Mark 13:19–22). God word will protect us from the enemy.

THE WORD DIVIDES SOUL AND SPIRIT

"For the word of God is quick and powerful, and sharper than any twoedged sword, piercing even to the dividing asunder of soul and spirit, and of the joints and marrow, and is a discerner of the thoughts and intents of the heart" (Hebrews 4:12).

Whatever God says is full of living power: it is sharper than the sharpest dagger, cutting swift and deep into our innermost thoughts and desires with all their parts, exposing us for what we really are. Because the word is so powerful we must be careful to know how to use the word. The word will keep us from sin: "Thy word have I hid in my heart that I might not sin against thee" (Psalms 119:11). The word is directions: "Thy word is a lamp unto my feet, and a light unto my path" (Psalms 119:105). The word is Truth: "Sanctify them through thy truth: thy word is truth" (John 17:17). The word will last forever: "But the word of the Lord endureth for ever" (I Peter 1:25). "In the beginning was the Word, and the Word was with God, and the Word was God. And the Word was made flesh and dwelt among us, (and we beheld His glory, the glory as of the only begotten of the Father) full of grace and truth" (John 1:1, 14). Let us commit ourselves to walk in the word because the Word is God. "So shall my word be that goeth forth out of my mouth: it shall not return unto me void, but it shall accomplish that which I please, and it shall prosper in the thing whereto I sent it" (Isaiah 55:11).

HE GAVE THEM THEIR REQUEST

"And He gave them their request; but sent leaness into their soul" (Psalms 106:15).

It is so very easy to take our blessings for granted and forget to be grateful for whatever we have. The Israelites had become tired of the manna that was sent down from heaven. The manna was about the size of coriander seed, and looked like droplets of gum from the bark of a tree. The people crushed it into flour or pounded it in mortars, boiled it and the taste of it was like fresh oil. They began to wish for fish, cucumbers, melons, leeks, and onions. They complained about only having manna. "And Moses said, unto the Lord, Wherefore hast thou afflicted thy servant? And wherefore have I not found favour in thy sight, that thou layest the burden of all this people upon me?" (Numbers 11:11). Moses asked, the Lord where can I get flesh for all these people? They are continually asking me for flesh. Moses said, this load is too heavy for me. The Lord told Moses to gather seventy elders of Israel and I will put on them, the spirit that is on you. Then the Lord told Moses, to tell the people to sanctify themselves, because He was going to give them flesh to eat. Not one day, nor two days, not five days, not ten days, not twenty, but a whole month, because you have rejected the Lord that is among you. "And while the flesh was yet between their teeth, ere it was chewed, the wrath of the Lord was kindled against the people, and the Lord smote the people with a very great plague" (Numbers 11:33). So, "the Lord gave them their request; but sent leaness into their soul." Let us not murmur and complain, but be grateful, and the Lord will bless us according to His will, without sending leaness into our souls.

Chapter 21

LET THIS CUP PASS FROM ME,
A NEW COVENANT,
LEND UNTO THE LORD,
AMERRY HEART.

LET THIS CUP PASS FROM ME

"And He went a little further, and fell on His face, and prayed saying, O my Father, if it be possible, let this cup pass from me: nevertheless not as I will, but as thou wilt" (Matthew 26:39).

The greatest act of love was based on a decision. Because Jesus loved His Father and us so much He said, "Nevertheless not as I will, but as thou wilt" Jesus said, "My soul is exceeding sorrowful, even unto death" Jesus certainly was not happy about the sacrifice He had to pay, but His love for us, was greater than the sacrifice. Some people have the mistaken idea, that God will only ask us to do things, that we will be happy about doing. This is so far from the truth. (Hebrews 12:2), tells us "Looking unto Jesus the author and finisher of our faith; who for the joy that was set before Him endured the cross, despising the shame, and is set down at the right hand of the throne of God." Jesus died for the future blessing of seeing souls come into His father kingdom. Jesus said in (Matthew 16:24), "If any man will come after me, let him deny himself take up his cross and follow me. Because we are all self-centered, denying ourselves is the last thing we want to do. Let's get over the mistaken idea, that we are going to be overjoyed at doing everything God ask us to do. God is concerned about us, being in His perfect will and we should be also. God is looking at end results. So let us say as Jesus said, "Nevertheless not as I will, but as thou wilt."

A NEW COVENANT

"But this shall be the covenant that I will make with the house of Israel; After those days, saith the Lord, I will put my law in their inward parts, and write it in their hearts; and will be their God, and they shall be my people. And they shall teach no more every man his neighbour, and every man his brother, saying, Know the Lord: for they shall all know me, from the least of them unto the greatest of them, saith the Lord: for I will forgive their iniquity, and I will remember their sin no more" (Jeremiah 31:33, 34).

The Lord says, I will inscribe my laws upon their hearts, so that they shall want to honor me, then they shall truly be my people and I will be their God. It will no longer be necessary, to admonish one another to know the Lord, because everyone, both great and small, shall really know me and I will forgive and forget their sins. The old covenant was ratified by the blood of animals and was based upon the promise of the people, that they would keep God's law. But the new covenant is based on God's promise, to write His law in our hearts. It was ratified with the blood of Christ. (Exodus 24:5; Hebrews 9:19) According to this scripture Gods law will be put in our inward parts, and wrote on our hearts. We will not have to be taught, there will be no excuse for not knowing God. "For the wrath of God is revealed from heaven against all ungodliness and unrighteousness of men, who hold the truth in unrighteousness; Because that which may be known of God is manifest in them; for God hath shewed it unto them. For the invisible things of Him from the creation of the world are clearly seen, being understood by the things that are made, even His eternal power and Godhead; so that they are without excuse" (Romans 1:18–20).

LEND UNTO THE LORD

"He that hath pity upon the poor lendeth unto the Lord; and that which he hath given will he pay him again" (Proverbs 19:17).

The word pity in this scripture is an action word. The person that gives to the poor is lending to the Lord and the Lord will give back. Pity in its use here can be as strong as love. When we have pity in our hearts for a person we will do all that we can to help. The Lord's pity is love. "Like as a father pitieth his children, so the Lord pitieth them that fear Him" (Psalms 103:13). The Lord is tender and sympathetic to those who reverence Him. Sometime we like to make people wait, we say, let me think about it, when we already know we are able to meet the need. "Withhold not good from them to whom it is due, when it is in the power of thine hand to do it. Say not unto thy neighbour, Go, and come again, and tomorrow I will give; when thou hast it by thee" (Proverbs 3:27, 28). Giving is just another word for love and as we give to those in need God will repay with interest.

A MERRY HEART

"A merry heart doeth good like a medicine: but a broken spirit drieth the bones" (Proverbs 17:22).

A merry heart keeps the body well, but a broken spirit makes a person sick. It is wonderful to be blessed with a sense of humor. Years ago, I thought people who laughed at almost everything, were so silly, but I understand now that we are all wired differently. I wish now that I could see humor in more things. Laughter frees the body of all tension and stress and helps to keep us well. A broken spirit is caused by disappointments in our lives, a sadness or hopelessness whether justified or not. So how do we have a merry heart? "And be not drunk with wine, wherein is excess, but be filled with the Spirit; Speaking to yourselves in psalms and hymns and spiritual songs, singing and making melody in your heart to the Lord; Giving thanks always for all things unto God and the Father in the name of our Lord Jesus Christ" (Ephesians 5:18–20). The key to a merry heart is God. If we put God word first, we can have everything else. Accept Christ, be filled with the spirit, by faith speak to yourself in psalms, and spiritual songs, singing and making melody in your heart, to the Lord, and giving thanks always for all things to God, and the Father, in the name of our Lord Jesus Christ. God can make all things right, He can change a broken spirit into a merry heart if we will only believe Him. "Jesus said unto him, if thou canst believe, all things are possible to him that believeth" (Mark 9:23).

Chapter 22

SPEAK WITH GRACE,
JESUS CHRIST AND HIM CRUCIFIED.

SPEAK WITH GRACE

"Let your speech be always with grace, seasoned with salt, that ye may know how ye ought to answer every man" (Colossians 4:6).

Grace always originates in the heart of God. Grace cannot be worked up, it must be prayed down from heaven. We can speak with grace only if our lives are filled with grace. How does this happen? Through a daily living connection with the source of all grace, through understanding how grace has been poured out upon us. "And the Word was made flesh, and dwelt among us, (and we beheld His glory, the glory as of the only begotten of the Father,) full of grace and truth. And of His fulness have all we received, and grace for grace" (John 1:14, 16). When we keep this great truth before us, that we have been recipients of grace, recieved from God through Christ, grace that we absolutely do not deserve, only then can we begin to speak with grace to others. Often times, we might be in a position where a firm word is needed, but even then it's not what we say, it is how we say it, the manner and the tone in which we speak. Our words can either reflect grace, or our own selfish nature. Even when we have been mistreated, the Lord desires that we respond with words of grace rather than words of rebuke or retaliation.

JESUS CHRIST AND HIM CRUCIFIED

"And I brethren, when I came to you, came not with excellency of speech or of wisdom, declaring unto you the testimony of God. For I determined not to know anything among you, save Jesus Christ, and Him crucified. And I was with you in

weakness and in fear, and much trembling. And my speech and my preaching was not with enticing words of man's wisdom, but in the demonstration of the Spirit and of power" (I Corinthians 2:1–4).

Paul didn't preach lofty words and brilliant ideas in God's message. He lifted up Jesus and His death on the cross. Paul spoke with God's power. He had no confidence in himself, because he was weak, timid, and he trembled. We must never let fear, prevent us from doing what the Lord wants us to do. His preaching was plain without human wisdom. However, his preaching was powerful because the Holy Spirit's power was in his words. The same Holy Spirit, who placed His seal of approval upon the preaching of Paul, will enable humble servants of Christ, in our generation, to also speak with a demonstration of divine power. Speaking in the power of the Holy Spirit, is not limited to preaching. God intends that all our speech be delivered with a demonstration of divine power. If we are speaking in the power of the Holy Spirit, our words, our tone, and our message will reflect the attributes, of the spirit that are made manifest, in lives touched by the Holy Spirit.

Chapter 23

VENGEANCE IS MINE,
ESTEEMED HIS WORD,
GUARD THINE EYES,
CONFESS AND BELIEVE.

VENGEANCE IS MINE

"Dearly beloved, avenge not yourselves, but rather give place unto wrath: for it is written, vengeance is mine, I will repay, saith the Lord" (Romans 12:19).

When we are angry and make plans to pay another back, we give place to the devil to tempt us. Therefore, God is unable to avenge us. "Be ye angry, and sin not: let not the sun go down upon your wrath: Neither give place to the devil" (Ephesians 4:26, 27). Give the angry to God, don't nurse a grudge get over it quickly. God will give you the strength to forgive and help you to deal with the memory, in a proper way. We must realize when we forgive, it does not mean that we will forget the incident, but when we allow God's forgiveness to work through us, we will be able to think about it without wanting to do harm. When God repays we are not to be happy! "Rejoice not when thine enemy falleth, and let not thine heart be glad when he stumbleth: Lest the Lord see it, and it displease Him, and He turn away His wrath from him." (Proverbs 24:17, 18). God is the only one, who can give us the love we need, that we won't rejoice when our enemy falls. "But I say unto you, Love your enemies, bless them that curse you, do good to them that hate you, and pray for them which despitefully use you, and persecute you; That you may be the children of your Father which is in heaven: for He maketh His sun to rise on the evil and on the good, and sendeth rain on the just and on the unjust" (Matthew 5:44, 45). God will enable you to do this, He won't ask us to do anything, that we can not do in His power.

ESTEEMED HIS WORDS

"Neither have I gone back from the commandments of His lips; I have esteemed the words of His mouth more than my necessary food." (Job 23:12).

Job complains to God, he says my punishment is far more than I deserve, I wish that I could find God I would go and talk to Him. However, in all of Job's complaining he says, I have not refused His commandments I have treasured the words of His mouth more than my daily food. Job was a very rich man, and although he did not belong to the people of Israel, he worshiped the Lord and was an upright person. The devil accused Job of serving God only because God was blessing him. God agreed to let the devil take away Job's wealth, children and his health to see if he would remain faithful to Him. Job did remain faithful. Job never understood why he suffered; he felt bitter, but he never rejected God or turned away from Him. Job was convinced that God would deliver him. My favorite scripture in the book of Job says: "Though He slay me, yet will I trust in Him: but I will maintain mine own ways before Him" (Job 13:15). Job trusted God. If only we would trust God, the way Job did, what a different world this would be. The book of Job also shows us the blessing of praying for those who despitefully use us. "And the Lord turned the captivity of Job, when he prayed for his friends: also the Lord gave Job twice as much as he had before" (Job 42:10).

GUARD THINE EYES

"I will set no wicked thing before mine eyes: I hate the work of them that turn aside; it shall not cleave to me" (Psalms 101:3).

"The light of the body is the eye: therefore when thine eye is single, thy whole body also is full of light; but when thine eye is evil, thy body also is full of darkness" (Luke 11:34).

Our eyes light up our inward being. A pure eye lets sunshine into your soul. A lustful eye shuts out the light and plunges you into darkness. David says, I will not look at any vile, vulgar, or base things, he despised the work of faithless men. Oh if only our christian men would speak as David spoke, there would be no room for pornography, it would not be breaking up so many homes today. How do we keep the right things before our eyes? "My son, let not them depart from thine eyes: keep sound wisdom and discretion: So shall they be life unto thy soul, and grace to thy neck" (Proverbs 3:21, 22). Wisdom will keep the wicked thing from our eyes. And where do we get wisdom? "The fear of the Lord is the beginning of wisdom: a good understanding have all they that do His commandments: His praise endureth for ever" (Psalms 111:10). The fear of the Lord gives us wisdom to look at what is wholesome.

CONFESS AND BELIEVE

"That if thou shalt confess with thy mouth the Lord Jesus, and shalt believe in thine heart that God hath raised Him from the dead, thou shalt be saved. For with the heart man believeth unto righteousness; and with the mouth confession is made unto salvation" (Romans 10:9, 10).

We must make a confession with our mouth that Jesus is our Lord and believe in our heart (mind) that God hath raised Jesus from the dead. Our belief in the heart (mind) makes us righteous and by our confession we are saved. What a great gift of salvation we have received from God. It is so simply that many people fail to understand. There are some things that we can't figure out, we just have to accept by faith and rejoice in it. "For the preaching of the cross is to them that perish foolishness; but unto us which are saved it is the power of God. For it is written, I will destroy the wisdom of the wise, and will bring to nothing the understanding of the prudent. Because the foolishness of God is wiser than men; and the weakness of God is stronger than men" (I Corinthians 1:18, 19, 25). The bible shows us a beautiful conversion in (Acts 16:25–33). "And at midnight Paul and Silas prayed, and sang praises unto God: and the prisoners heard them. And suddenly there was a great earthquake, so that the foundations of the prison were shaken: and immediately all the doors were opened, and every one's bands were loosed. And the keeper of the prison awaking out of his sleep, and seeing the prison doors open, he drew out his sword, and would have killed himself, supposing that the prisoners had been fled. But Paul cried with a loud voice, saying, Do thyself no harm: for we are all here. Then he called for a light, and sprang in, and came trembling, and fell down before Paul and Silas, And brought them out, and said, Sirs, what must I do to be saved? And they said, Believe on the Lord Jesus Christ, and thou shalt be saved, and thy house. And they spake unto him the word of the Lord, and to all that were in his house. And he took them the same hour of the night, and washed their stripes; and was baptized, he and all his, straightway." (Verse 25) says, the prisoners heard them. They were praying and singing praises in a time when many would have been complaining. What a wonderful testimony Paul and Silas were for the prisoners. (Verse 32) lets us know that we should be taught, and get an understanding of the gift of salvation, before we are baptised.

Chapter 24

GOD WILL REVIVE US,
EVERLASTING LOVE,
BE DILIGENT,
CHRIST DIED FOR US.

GOD WILL REVIVE US

"Though I walk in the midst of trouble, thou wilt revive me: thou shalt stretch forth thine hand against the wrath of mine enemies, and thy right hand shall save me" (Psalms 138:7).

When we walk through trials God keeps us strong, His hand is against the evil of our enemies and His power will save us, no one can stand against Him. At sometime in our lives we will "walk in the midst of trouble". How comforting it is to know that God, will be with us in our troubles. It is not a matter of if they come, it is when, for they surely will. He will also revive us because sometimes it seems as if all our strength has been sapped away by a sponge. "Jesus answered and said unto her, Whosoever drinketh of this water shall thirst again: But whosoever drinketh of the water that I shall give him shall never thirst; but the water that I shall give him shall be in him a well of water springing up into everlasting life" (John 4:13, 14). This "well of water springing up into everlasting life," will be able to keep us revived, no matter what trial we are going through. This promise of everlasting life is enough to keep us revived.

EVERLASTING LOVE

"The Lord hath appeared of old unto me, saying, yea, I have loved thee with an everlasting love: therefore with loving kindness have I drawn thee" (Jeremiah 31:3).

The Lord will never stop loving us no matter what we do. Because of His love for us, He made us free moral agents, we have a choice, to accept Him or reject Him. He didn't want to make us like robots, He wanted us to choose to love Him. Therefore, He never forces us to obey Him, never herds or drive us like cattle; He uses only love to Win us. The greatest attraction that He used was His suffering and death on the cross. "O my Father, if this cup may not pass away from me except I drink it, thy will be done" (Matthew 26:42). He drank the cup of death for you and me and was separated from His Father. "And about the ninth hour Jesus cried with a loud voice, saying, E-li, E-li, la-ma sa-bach-tha-ni? That is to say, My God, my God, why hast thou forsaken me? Jesus took on Him all the sins of the world. It is awesome when we understand that the Father gave the best that heaven had to offer! "Let this mind be in you, which was also in Christ Jesus: Who, being in the form of God, thought it not robbery to be equal with God: But made himself of no reputation, and took upon Him the form of a servant, and was made in the likeness of men: And being found in fashion as a man, He humbled Himself, and became obedient unto death, even the death of the cross" (Philippians 2:5–8) With this kind of love who wouldn't be drawn to God.

BE DILIGENT

"The soul of the sluggard desireth, and hath nothing: but the soul of the diligent shall be made fat" (Proverbs 13:4).

The lazy person sits and day dream all day wishing that he might win the lottery or that he might inherit money from his rich uncle. He hasn't read "But seek ye first the kingdom of God, and His righteousness; and all these things shall be added unto you" (Matthew 6:33). God's word is true, He will do what ever, He says He will do. All of the things we desire will be added unto us if we would only seek first the kingdom of God, and His righteousness. However, the diligent person shall be made fat because he expects to find good. "He that diligently seeketh good procureth favor" (Proverbs 11:27).

When we search for good we find God's favor and the resourceful person will be richly supplied.

CHRIST DIED FOR US

"But God commendeth His love toward us, in that while we were yet sinners, Christ died for us" (Romans 5:8).

God showed His great love toward us, when we were hopeless, and helpless we were deep in sin and had no way out. We had the nature of Adam, our father. And we liked what we were doing. But God looked down on us and had mercy on us and sent His Son at the right time. "But when the fulness of the time was come, God sent forth His Son, made of a woman, made under the law, To redeem them that were under the law, that we might receive the adoption of sons" (Galatians 4:4). God does everything when the time is right. He is never late always on time. He didn't say I am going to wait until they stop sinning because He knew we were too weak to help ourselves. "For what the law could not do, in that it was weak through the flesh, God sending His own Son in the likeness of sinful flesh, and for sin, condemned sin in the flesh. That the righteousness of the law might be fulfilled in us, who walk not after the flesh, but after the spirit" (Romans 8:3, 4). We are not saved from sin's grasp by knowing the commandments of God, because we couldn't keep them, but God put into effect a different plan to save us. He sent His own Son in a human body just like ours, except ours are sinful, and destroyed sin's control over us, by giving Himself as a sacrifice for our sins.

Chapter 25

THE DUST RETURNS TO THE EARTH, OWE NO MAN ANYTHING, THE DESTRUCTION OF THE FLESH, GODLINESS AND CONTENTMENT.

THE DUST RETURNS TO THE EARTH

"Then shall the dust return to the earth as it was: and the spirit shall return unto God who gave it" (Ecclesiastes 12:7).

The body returns to the dust again, and the spirit goes back to God, who gave it. The spirit of every person who dies whether righteous or wicked returns to God at death. "And the Lord God formed man of the dust of the ground, and breathed into his nostrils the breath of life; and man became a living soul "(Genesis 2:7). The spirit that returns to God at death is the breath of life. Nowhere in the bible does the spirit have any life, wisdom, or feeling after a person dies. A soul is a living being. A soul is always a combination of two things: body plus breath. A soul (person) cannot exist unless body and breath are combined. According to God's word, souls do die! We are souls, and souls die. "Behold, all souls are mine; as the soul of the father, so also the soul of the son is mine: the soul that sinneth, it shall die" (Ezekiel 18:4). Man is mortal (Job 4:17). Only God is immortal (I Timothy 6:15, 16). Body (dust) minus breath (spirit) equals death (no soul)."All that are in the graves shall hear His voice, And shall come forth" (John 5:28, 29). "For David is not ascended into the heavens" (Acts 2:29, 34). "The living know that they shall die: but the dead know not any thing, neither have they any more a reward; for the memory of them is forgotten. Also their love and their hatred, and their envy, is now perished; neither have they any more a portion for ever in any thing that is done under the sun" (Ecclesiastes 9:5).

OWE NO MAN ANYTHING

"Owe no man any thing, but to love one another: for he that loveth another hath fulfilled the law" (Romans 13:8).

"Master, which is the great commandment in the law? Jesus said unto him, thou shalt love the Lord thy God with all thy heart, and with all thy soul, and with all thy mind. This is the first and great commandment. And the second is like unto it, Thou shalt love thy neighbour as thyself. On these two commandments hang all the law and the prophets" (Matthew 22:36–40). Nothing works without the love of God in our hearts. "And hope maketh not ashamed; because the love of God is shed abroad in our hearts by the Holy Ghost which is given unto us" (Romans 5:5) When God's love is shed abroad in our hearts, we know that all is well, as we feel this love within us. "For all the law is fulfilled in one word, even in this; Thou shalt love thy nieghbour as thyself" (Galatians 5:14).

THE DESTRUCTION OF THE FLESH

"In the name of our Lord Jesus Christ, when ye are gathered together, and my spirit, with the power of our Lord Jesus Christ, To deliver such an one unto satan for the destruction of the flesh, that the spirit may be saved in the day of the Lord Jesus" (I Corinthians 5:4, 5).

Paul wrote this letter to the Corinthians church. He told them, that he had heard, that some of them, were behaving worst than the Gentiles. A man is living in sin, with his father's wife! The church should be mourning in sorrow, and shame. This man should be removed from your membership. Call a meeting of the church, and cast this man out, into the devil's hands to punish him, in the hope that his soul will be saved, when our Lord Jesus Christ returns. What a terrible thing it is that you are boasting about your purity, and let this kind of thing happen. Don't you realize that if even one person is allowed to go on sinning, soon all will be affected? Remove this man from among you, so that you can stay pure. Scripture tells the church, how to deal with members in the church, that trespass against one another. "Moreover if thy brother shall trespass against thee, go and tell him his fault between thee and him alone: if he shall hear thee, thou hast gained thy brother. But if he will not hear thee, then take with thee one or two more, that in the mouth of two or three witnesses every word may be established. And if he shall neglect to hear them, tell it unto the church: but if he neglect to hear the church, let him be unto thee as an heathen man and a publican." (Matthew 18:15–17).

GODLINESS AND CONTENTMENT

"But godliness with contentment is great gain. For we brought nothing into this world, and it is certain we can carry nothing out. And having food and raiment let us be therewith content" (I Timothy 6:6–8).

Godliness is having the character of God, that can be summed up in one word Love. Godliness and contentment is an unbeatable team it certainly is great gain. We should not work hard to be rich, because we are going to leave it all here for someone else to enjoy. "He heapeth up riches, and knoweth not who shall gather them" (Psalms 39:6) When we have godliness, we are content, in all situations. Our contentment is based on our confidence in our Lord Jesus Christ, He is the one who strengthens us, our rock when everything is shifting sand, our surety when everything else is uncertain. Apart from Jesus there is no true contentment "For the Lord shall be thy confidence, and shall keep thy foot from being taken" (Proverbs 3:26). What greater confidence, do we need other than the Lord, He is omnipotence (having absolute power), omnipresent (everywhere at the same time), and omniscient (knowing everything).

Chapter 26

KEEP HIS COMMANDMENTS,
THE POTTER'S HAND,
BARE OUR SINS, HUMBLE YOURSELVES.

KEEP HIS COMMANDMENTS

"And whatsoever we ask, we receive of Him, because we keep His commandments, and do those things that are pleasing in His sight. And this is His commandment, That we should believe on the name of His Son Jesus Christ, and love one another, as He gave us commandment. And He that keepeth His commandments dwelleth in Him, and He in him, and hereby we know that He abideth in us, by the Spirit which he hath given us" (I John 3:22–24).

We receive of Him because we keep His commandments, and do those things that are pleasing in His sight, believe on the name of His Son, and love one another. Because we do those things that are pleasing in His sight, we receive whatsoever we ask of Him. God can freely give us what we ask for, because we will only ask for the things that we know will be pleasing to Him. We must love one another. "For all the law is fulfilled in one word, even in this; Thou shalt love thy neighbour as thyself" (Galatians 5:14). We know that if we keep His commandments we dwell in Him. "If ye keep my commandments ye shall abide in my love; even as I have kept my Fathers commandments, and abide in His love" (John 15:10). When we are obedient we are living in His love, just as Jesus obeyed His Father and live in His love also.

THE POTTER'S HAND

"O house of Israel, cannot I do with you as this potter? Saith the Lord. Behold, as the clay is in the potter's hand, so are ye in mine hand, O house of Israel" (Jeremiah 18:6).

The Lord told Jeremiah to go to the potter's house and I will speak to you. As Jeremiah watched the potter mold the clay, the jar did not please him. So he formed it into another, as it seemed best to him. The Lord spoke the words of the above scripture to Jeremiah. He said, why can't I do to you as the potter has done to his clay? As the clay is in the potter's hand, so are you in my hand. The Lord desires us, to be like Him, but because God gave us a free will He can not and will not force His will on us. He can only draw us by His lovingkindness. "The Lord hath appeared of old unto me, saying, Yea, I have loved thee with an everlasting love: therefore with lovingkindness have I drawn thee" (Jeremiah 31:3). We must allow the Lord, to remake us as the potter did the clay and we can, as we surrender our lives to Him. "Submit yourselves therefore to God. "Resist the devil, and he will flee from you" (James 4:7). We submit to God by obedience to His word. We resist the devil by using God's word. Therefore, he will flee, and we are free to surrender all to God.

BARE OUR SINS

"Who His own self bare our sins in His own body on the tree, that we, being dead to sins, should live unto righteousness: by whose stripes ye were healed. For ye were as sheep going astray; but are now returned unto the Shepherd and Bishop of your souls" (I Peter 2:24, 25).

Jesus took on Himself all the sin of each person in the world whether that person chose to accept Him or not. He gave us a choice, not only to eternal life, but an abundant life here on earth, a choice not to be slaves to sin, and healing for our bodies. "The thief cometh not, but for to steal, and to kill, and to destroy: I am come that they might have life, and that they might have it more abundantly" (John 10:10). Jesus suffered greatly before His death. "And they stripped Him, and put on Him a scarlet robe. And when they had platted a crown of thorns, they put it upon His head, and a reed in His right hand: and they bowed the knee before Him, and mocked Him,saying, Hail, King of the Jews! And they spit upon Him, and took the reed, and smote Him on the head"

(Matthew 27:28–30). Jesus death bridged the gap between the sinner and God. "Looking unto Jesus the author and finisher of our faith; who for the joy set before Him endured the cross, scorning its shame, and sat down at the right hand of the throne of God" (Hebrews 12:2). His joy was in knowing that His sacrifice would give us a choice to live an abundant life here on earth and spend eternity with Him.

HUMBLE YOURSELVES

"If I shut up heaven that there be no rain, or if I command the locust to devour the land, or if I send pestilence among my people. If my people, which are called by my name, shall humble themselves, and pray, and seek my face, and turn from their wicked ways; then will I hear from heaven, and will forgive their sin, and will heal their land" (II Chronicles 7:14).

The Lord says, "If I shut up heaven that there be no rain, or if I command the locust to devour the land, or if I send pestilence among my people" Then, all my people need to do is humble themselves, pray, seek my face, turn from their wicked ways and I will hear from heaven, and will forgive their sin, and will heal their land. These are the words that the Lord spoke to Solomon, after he had dedicated the new temple and celebrated the festival seven days. He also said, "But if ye turn away, and forsake my statutes and my commandments, which I have set before you, and shall go and serve other gods, and worship them; Then will I pluck them up by the roots out of my land which I have given them; and this house, which I have sanctified for my name, will I cast out of my sight, and will make it to be a proverb and a byword among all nations" (II Chronicles 7:19, 20). These words are for us today as well. In our troubled world, we must humble ourselves, pray, seek His face, turn from our wicked ways and our sins, that are many will be forgiven and our land will be healed. The Lord wants to bless us more than we want to be blessed. He is just waiting for us to turn back to Him and worship Him only.

Chapter 27

GIVING WILLINGLY, BE FAITHFUL, GLORY IN HIM, NO CONDEMNATION IN CHRIST, THE GREAT COMMISSION, WHO IS YOUR MASTER.

GIVING WILLINGLY

"I know also, my God, that thou triest the heart, and hast pleasure in uprightness. As for me, in the uprightness of mine heart I have willingly offered all these things: and now have I seen with joy thy people, which are present here, to offer willingly unto thee" (I Chronicles 29:17).

David told the people what he had given for the building of the temple then he asked the people "Who then is willing to consecrate his service this day unto the Lord?" And they all offered willingly. Afterward the people rejoiced, because they offered willingly with perfect heart to the Lord and David rejoiced with them. And then David offered this beautiful prayer to God."O Lord God of our Father Israel, praise your name for ever and ever! Yours is the mighty power and glory and victory and majesty. Everything in the heavens and earth is yours, O Lord, and this is your kingdom. We adore you as being in control of everything. Riches and honor come from you alone, and you are the Ruler of all mankind; your hand controls power and might, and it is at your discretion that men are made great and given strength. O our God we thank you and praise your glorious name, but who am I and who are my people that we should be permitted to give anything to you? Everything we have has come from you, and we only give you what is already yours!" (I Chronicles 29:10–14 LB). And God does test the heart and is pleased with integrity. And

He blesses us above measure when we open up our hearts and give willingly to Him.

BE FAITHFUL

"He that is faithful in that which is least is faithful also in much: and he that is unjust in the least is unjust also in much. If therefore ye have not been faithful in the unrighteous mammon, who will commit to your trust the true riches. And if ye have not been faithful in that which is another man's who shall give you that which is your own?" (Luke 16:10–12).

Unless we are honest in small matters, we won't be honest with large ones. If we cheat even a little, we won't be honest with greater responsibilities. And if we are untrustworthy about worldly wealth, who will trust us with the true riches of heaven. The parable of the talents is a good example of being faithful in what is least. "For the kingdom of heaven is as a man travelling into a far country, who called his own servants, and delivered unto them his goods. And unto one he gave five talents, to another two, and to another one; to every man according to his several ability; and straightway took his journey" (Matthew 25:14, 15). The one with the five talents invested and gained five more talents, the one with two talents invested and received two more talents, and the one that received one talent went and buried his money in the ground. After a long time the master returned and called them to account for his money. He praised both servants who had gained talents and said I will make you ruler over many things. To the one that had buried his talent he said, give me your talent and I will give it to the servant with the ten talents. "For unto every one that hath shall be given, and he shall have abundance: but from him that hath not shall be taken away even that which he hath" (Matthew 25:29). the man who uses well what he is given shall be given more and he shall have abundance. But from the man who is unfaithful, even what responsibilities he has shall be taken from him. We must use whatever God gives us, that we may be given more.

GLORY IN HIM

"Thus saith the Lord, Let not the wise man glory in his wisdom, neither let the mighty man glory in his might, let not the rich man glory in his riches: But let him that glorieth glory in this, that he understandeth and knoweth me, that I am the Lord which exercise lovingkindness, judgment, and righteousness, in the earth: for in these things I delight, saith the Lord" (Jeremiah 9:23, 24).

All good things come from God. Therefore, we should give Him the glory for what ever we have. He gives wisdom: "For the Lord giveth wisdom: out of His mouth cometh knowledge and understanding" (Proverbs 2:6). He gives might: "And in thine hand is power and might" (I Chronicles 29:12). He gives riches: "The blessings of the Lord, it maketh rich, and He addeth no sorrow with it" (Proverbs 10:22). We should also glory in the fact that He understands and know us. "For He knoweth our frame; He remembereth that we are dust" (Psalms 103:14). We should glory in the fact that He exercise lovingkindness: "Because thy lovingkindness is better than life, my lips shall praise thee". We should glory in the fact that He exercise judgement: "For we must all appear before the judgment seat of Christ; that every one may receive the things done in his body, according to that he hath done, whether it be good or bad" (II Corinthians 5:10). We should glory in the fact that He exercises righteousness: "Even the righteousness of God which is by faith of Jesus Christ unto all and upon all them that believe: for there is no difference: For all have sinned and come short of the glory of God" (Romans 3:22, 23). And last but not least we should glorify God because: "For ye are bought with a price: therefore glorify God in your body, and in your spirit, which are God's"(I Corinthians 7:20).

NO CONDEMNATION IN CHRIST

"There is therefore now no condemnation to them which are in Christ Jesus, who walk not after the flesh, but after the Spirit. For the law of the Spirit of life in Christ Jesus hath made me free from the law of sin and death". (Romans 8:1, 2).

For what the law was powerless to do in that it was weakened by the sinful nature, God did by sending His own Son in the likeness of sinful man to be a sin offering. And so He condemned sin in sinful man, in order that the righteous requirement of the law might be fully met in us, who do not live according to the sinful nature but according to the Spirit. Now, we don't have to listen to the devil condemnation, telling us that we are sinful, because Jesus condemned sin in the flesh by His death on the cross. "For what saith the scripture? Abraham believed God, and it was counted unto him for righteousness. Now to him that worketh is the reward not reckoned of grace, but of debt. But to him that worketh not, but believeth on Him that justifieth the ungodly, his faith is counted for righteousness" (Romans 4:3–5). Because Abraham believed God, his sins were canceled and he was declared righteous. Abraham didn't earn his right to heaven by his good works, because salvation is a gift; if a person could earn salvation by being good it would not be a gift. However, it is a gift, given to those who believe on the Son of God.

THE GREAT COMMISSION

"And this gospel of the kingdom shall be preached in all the world for a witness unto all nations; and then shall the end come". (Matthew 24:14).

We have been given the "Great Commission" "Go ye therefore, and teach all nations, baptizing them in the name of the Father, and of the Son, and of the Holy Ghost" (Matthew 28:19). So we have a work before us, we all should be about our Father's business and that is soul winning. It does not mean that everybody we witness to will surrender at that time, but we are to plant seeds. "I have planted, Apollos watered; but God gave the increase, So neither is he that planteth anything, neither he that watereth; but God that giveth the increase" (I Corinthians 3:6, 7). As we are obedient to plant seeds God will add souls to His kingdom. Many are speculating about the time of Jesus return but we will know: "For the Lord Himself shall descend from heaven with a shout, with the voice of the archangel, and with the trump of

God: and the dead in Christ shall rise first" (I Thessalonians 4:16). Then and only then will we (All) know. However, the most important question is, are you ready? (For He saith, I have heard thee in a time accepted, and in the day of salvation have I succoured thee: behold, now is the accepted time; behold, now is the day of salvation). (II Corinthians 6:2). We may not be here Tomorrow. His return is today for each of us. Surrender your heart to Jesus today and then you will be ready for His return.

WHO IS YOUR MASTER

"No servant can serve two masters: for either he will hate the one, and love the other; or else he will hold to one, and despise the other. Ye cannot serve God and mammon" (Luke 16:13).

We have the choice of choosing our own master. The one that we give most of our time and energy to will be our master. Your master will be God or money."But they that will be rich fall into temptation and a snare, and into many foolish and hurtful lusts, which drown men in destruction and perdition. For the love of money is the root of all evil: which while some coveted after, they have erred from the faith, and pierced themselves through with many sorrows". (I Timothy 6:9, 10). People who want to get rich fall into temptation and a trap and into many foolish and harmful desires that plunge them into ruin and destruction. The love of money is a root of all kinds of evil. Some people, eager for money, have wandered from the faith and pierced themselves with grief, Instead of serving money that can't save, why not choose God? Because: "But as it is written, Eye hat not seen, nor ear heard neither have entered in the heart of man, the things which God hath prepared for them that love Him. But God hath revealed them unto us by His Spirit: for the Spirit searcheth all things, yea, the deep things of God." (I Corinthians 2:9, 10).

Chapter 28

THE TEMPLE OF THE HOLY GHOST, HIS WILL ONLY.

THE TEMPLE OF THE HOLY GHOST

"What? know ye not that your body is the temple of the Holy Ghost which is in you, which ye have of God, and ye are not your own? For ye are bought with a price: therefore glorify God in your body, and in your spirit, which are God's" (I Corinthians 6:19, 20).

Our body does not belong to us it was bought with a price, a great price, the precious blood of Christ. Our spiritual lives are not separate from the lives we live in the physical realm. What happens to us in the physical realm affect our spiritual lives. If God speak to us about becoming a vegetarian, to fast, or to lose excess weight, we will be affected both spiritually and physically because our bodies will not become diseased, affecting our ability to be used of God. God want us to stop doing things, that have negatives results in our spiritual lives. He want us to stop overeating and begin to exercise, to be careful what we look at and what we hear. "The eye is not satisified with seeing, nor the ear filled with hearing." (Ecclesiates 1:8). The eye is not satisified with just seeing, it has to follow through with the action and the ear is never satisified with hearing it must hear more. "I will set no wicked thing before mine eyes" (Psalms 101:3). The ear is not satisified with the truth of the gospel. "And they shall turn away their ears from the truth, and shall be turned unto fables" (II Timothy 4:4). Our mouth, eyes, and ears are the parts of our bodies that keep us from glorifying God. We can only glorify God by walking in the spirit. "This I say then, walk in the spirit, and ye shall not fulfill the lust of the flesh"

(Galatians 5:16). The Holy Spirit will help you take control of your body and be able to glorify God.

HIS WILL ONLY

"And the multitude sat about Him, and they said unto Him, Behold, thy mother and thy brethren without seek for thee. And He answered them, saying who is my mother, or my brethren?" (Mark 3:32, 33).

After Jesus asked them the question who is my mother and my brother? He said, "For whosoever shall do the will of God, the same is my brother, and my sister, and mother" (Matthew 12:50). Isn't it wonderful to know that when we do the will of God we become, as close to Him as, His brother, sister and mother? To do God's will He must be first in our lives. He must be Lord over all of our priorities. Doing the Father's will was His number one priority. His plan was to discover the Father's will and do it. He must be Lord of our thoughts. "Casting down imaginations and every high thing that exalteth itself against the knowlede of God, and bringing into captivity every thought to the obedience of christ" (I Corinthians 10:5). Every thought must be brought into the obedience of the word of God. We must submit all our desires to the will of God. "For I come down from heaven, not to do mine own will, but the will of Him that sent me" (John 6:38). He must be Lord of our prayers. "And this is the confidence that we have in Him, that, if we ask anything according to His will, He heareth us: And if we know that He hear us whatsoever we ask, we know that we have the petitions that we disired of Him." (I John 5:14, 15). Jesus says, if you are doing my will, you are as close to me as my brother, sister or mother!

Chapter 29

WE SHALL BE JUDGED,
GOD OF GRACE,
ONE HEART,
THE SPIRIT POURED OUT

WE SHALL BE JUDGED

"For the time is come that judgement must begin at the house of God: and if it first begin at us, what shall the end be of them that obey not the gospel of God? And if the righteous scarcely be saved, where shall the ungodly and sinner appear? Wherefore let them that suffer according to the will of God commit the keeping of their souls to Him in well doing, as unto a faithful Creator". (I Peter 4:17–19).

We must all stand before Christ to be judged and have our lives open before Him. Each of us will receive whatever we deserve for the good or bad things we have done in our bodies. This scripture lets us know that if we suffer according to the will of God, we can commit the keeping of our souls to God. We know that the wrath of God will be upon the ungodly and the sinner, so we that are righteous should be praying and witnessing to as many unbelievers as possible, because time is running out. "I must work the works of Him that sent me, while it is day; the night cometh, when no man can work." (John 9:4). Jesus left us the great commission (Matthew 28:19) and we should be working while we have time because the night will soon be here and then no man can work. We must pray and ask God to give us a love for people, a desire that everybody be saved. "The Lord is not slack concerning His promise, as some men count slackness; but is longsuffering to us-ward, not willing that any should perish, but that all should come to repentance" (II Peter 3:10). The Lord is longsuffering, He give us so much time to repent and come to Him, because He loves us so much and does not want to see any perish. We must have that same love in our hearts. We can never feel that we have done enough and cease our work, because the word says, "And ye shall be hated of all men for my name's sake: but he that endureth to the end shall be saved". (Matthew 10:22).

GOD OF GRACE

"But the God of all grace, who hath called us into His eternal glory by Christ Jesus, after that ye have suffered a while, make you perfect, stablish, strengthen, settle you" (I Peter 5:10).

This suffering is all part of the work God has given you. "For what glory is it, if, when ye be buffeted for your faults, ye shall take it patiently? But if, when ye do well and suffer for it, ye take it patiently this is acceptable with God. For even hereunto were ye called: because Christ also suffered for us, leaving us an example, that ye should follow His steps: Who did no sin, neither was guile found in His mouth". (I Peter 2:20–22). After we have proved ourselves through suffering, God will be able to set us firmly in place, and make us strong forever. Jesus said, "If any man will come after me, let him deny himself, and take up his cross daily, and follow me. For whosoever will save his life shall lose it: but whosoever will lose his life for my sake, the same shall save it" (Luke 9:23, 24). We must put aside our own desires, conveniences, and suffer for the cause of Christ.

ONE HEART

"And I will give them one heart and I will put a new spirit within you; and I will take the stony heart out of their flesh, and will give them an heart of flesh: That they may walk in my statutes, and keep mine ordinances, and do them: and they shall be my people, and I will be their God". (Ezekiel 11:19, 20).

Ezekiel was a priest and a prophet. He had been taken away as a prisoner to Babylonia, where he lived among the other exiles from Judah. The Lord chose Ezekiel to be His prophet and to preach His message, not only to the exiles in Babylonia, but also to the people still living in Jerusalem. Ezekiel's ministry probably began around 593 B. C. during the last years of the kingdom of Judah, and ended sometime around 570 B.C. The lord told Israel, I will remove your heart of stone and give you a tender heart of love for me, so that you can obey my laws and be my people and I will be your God. This was a promise to Israel and it is a promise to us also. When we accept Christ, as our Lord and saviour, we receive a new heart that wants to keep His commandments. "Therefore if any man be in Christ, he is a new creature: old things are passed away; behold, all things are become new" (II Corinthians 5:17). When we become new creatures, we can walk in God's statutes, keep God ordinances, and receive His righteousness and true holiness. We are new on the inside, we no longer desire to do what we have done, to speak as we have spoken, and go where we have gone. Now we can be imitators of God walking in His love.

THE SPIRIT POURED OUT

"And it shall come to pass afterward, that I will pour out my spirit upon all flesh; and your sons and your daughters shall prophesy, your old men shall dream dreams, your young men shall see visions. And also upon the servants and upon the handmaids in those days will I pour out my spirit." (Joel 2:28, 29).

This prophecy was fulfilled in the book of Acts. "And suddenly there came a sound from heaven as of a rushing mighty wind, and it filled all the house where they were sitting. And there appeared unto them cloven tongues like as of fire, and it sat upon each of them. And they were all filled with the Holy Ghost, and began to speak with other tongues, as the Spirit gave them utterance. And there were dwelling at Jerusalem Jews, devout men, out of every nation under heaven. Now when this was noised abroad, they all came together, and were confounded, because that every man heard them speak in his own language" (Acts 2:2–6). Everyone in the upper room was filled with the Holy Ghost and began speaking in languages they had not learned. The Holy Ghost gave them this ability. How can this be? They exclaimed, for these men are all from Galilee, and yet, we hear them speaking all the native languages of the lands where we were born. And we all hear these men telling in our own languages about the mighty miracles of God! It was the day of Pentecost. Which was the Jewish Feast of Weeks. Which fell on the fiftieth day after the Feast of the Passover.

Chapter 30

MAKE THY NAME GREAT.

MAKE THY NAME GREAT

"Now the Lord had said unto Abram, Get thee out of thy country, and from thy kindred, and from thy father's house, unto a land that I will shew thee: And I will make of thee a great nation, and I will bless thee, and make thy name great; and thou shalt be a blessing: And I will bless them that bless thee, and curse him that curseth thee: and in thee shall all families of the earth be blessed" (Genesis 12:1–3).

When God told Abram to leave his country he was faced with a decision whether to obey or disobey. God did not tell him where he was going. He said, I want you to go to a land that I will show you. I don't believe that God had road maps for Abram saying, turn left here, go north here and south here. Abram had to listen to the spirit guidance. With the command to leave his home, Abram was given many promises. I will make thee a great nation, I will bless thee, make thy name great, thou shalt be a blessing, I will bless them that bless thee, curse him that curseth thee, and in thee shall all families of the earth be blessed. "Neither shall thy name any more be called Abram, but thy name shall be Abraham; for a father of many nations have I made thee. And I will make thee exceeding fruitful, and I will make nations of thee, and kings shall come out of thee. And I will establish my covenant between me and thee and thy seed after thee in their generations for an everlasting covenant, to be a God unto thee, and to thy seed after thee. And I will give unto thee, and to thy seed after thee, the land wherein thou art a stranger, all the land of Canaan for an everlasting possession; and I will be their God" (Genesis 17:5–8). What wonderful promises God gave Abraham! I believe that the promises were much greater than the trials.

Chapter 31

THE LORD PRESERVETH,
LOVE YOUR ENEMIES,
GRIEVE NOT THE HOLY SPIRIT.

THE LORD PRESERVETH

"The Lord preserveth all them that love Him: but all the wicked will He destroy" (Psalms 145:20).

Preserve means to maintain in existing state. God is the only one,who can perserve us. But there is something we must do. The verse says, "All them that love Him" we must love Him. How do we show our love for God? It is not that warm fuzzy feeling we have sometimes.That's not love! "If ye love me, keep my commandments" (John 14:15). We must Keep God's commandments, keeping God's commandments will cause us to do all the other things we should do. The Ten Commandments itself will preserve us because it is God in all of His character. Solomon said, "Let us hear the conclusion of the whole matter: Fear God, and keep His commandments: for this is the whole duty of man. For God shall bring every work into judgement, with every secret thing, whether it be good, or whether it be evil" (Ecclesiastes 12:13, 14). God is the one we must cling to with all our strength because he is our preserver. "Now unto Him that is able to keep you from falling, and to present you faultless before the presence of His glory with exceeding joy, To the only wise God our Saviour, be glory and majesty, dominion and power, both now and ever. Amen." (Jude 24).

LOVE YOUR ENEMIES

"Ye have heard that it hath been said, Thou shalt love thy neighbour, and hate thine ememy. But I say unto you, love your enemies, bless them that curse you, do good to them that hate you, and pray for them which despitefully use you, and persecute you; That ye may be the children of your Father which is in heaven: for He maketh His sun to rise on the evil and on the good, and sendeth rain on the just and on the unjust" (Matthew 5:43–45).

When God saves us, and fill us with His Holy Spirit, He enables us to love our enemies, bless them that curse us, do good to them that hate us, and pray for them which despitefull use and persecute us. God is love, and without being filled with God's love, we are unable to do these things, because of our old nature. "But the natural man receiveth not the things of the Spirit of God: for they are foolishness unto him: neither can he know them, because they are spiritually discerned" (I Cor. 2:14) . When we are able to do these things, it shows that we are the children of our Father, which is in heaven. Because He loves us all, He lets His sun rise on the evil, and the good, and lets it rain on the just, and on the unjust. If we love only the ones that love us, we are no different from the world, but when we can love our enemies, it shows that we have the love of God in us.

GRIEVE NOT THE HOLY SPIRIT

"And grieve not the Holy spirit of God, whereby ye are sealed unto the day of redemption" (Ephesians 4:20).

"There is one God; Father, Son, and Holy Spirit, a unity of three co-eternal Persons." There is one God (Deuteronomy 6:4) who exists as three Persons. This might not be simple, the bibical evidence for this truth is powerful. That we can't fully understand something, especially about the nature of God Himself, is not a reason to reject it. "God the eternal Spirit was active with the Father and the Son in Creation, incarnation, and redemption. He inspired the writers of Scripture. He filled Christ's life with power. He draws and convicts human beings; and those who respond He renews and transforms into the image of God. Sent by the Father and the Son to be always with His children, He extends spiritual gifts to the church, empowers it to bear witness concerning Christ, and in harmony with the Scriptures leads it into all truth. It was the Spirit who inspired the writers of the Scriptures (II Peter 1:21), when the Spirit speaks today, He will speak in accordance with His own inspired messages. Anything not in conformity with the Bible must therefore come from some source other than the Holy Spirit. The Bible presents the Holy Spirit as a distinct personality, one that has intelligence (John 14:26, 15:26, Romans 8:16), a will (Acts 16:7, I Corinthians 12:11), and affections (Ephesians 4:30). The Bible also attributes to the Holy Spirit actions that reveal personality. He is said to speak expressly (I Timothy 4:1), to send people on missions (Acts 10:19, 20), to prevent people from going places (Acts 16:7), to command people (Acts 11:12), to forbid actions (Acts 16:6), to call ministers of the gospel (Acts 13:2), to appoint them their spheres of duty (Acts 20:28), and to make intercession (Romans 8:26, 27). The doctrine of the personality of the Holy Spirit is of the highest importance. "If we think of the Holy Spirit only as an impersonal power or influence, then our thought will constantly be, how can I get hold of and use the Holy Spirit; but if we think of Him in the Biblical way as a divine person, infinitely wise, infinitely holy, infinitely tender, then our thought will constantly be, "How can the Holy Spirit get hold of and use me?" Alonzo J. Wearner, *Fundamentals of Bible Doctrine* (Washington, D.C.: Review and Herald Pub. Assoc., 1945), p. 39. The Holy Spirit wants to guide us into all truth, (John 16:13). We grieve the Holy Spirit when we do not obey His leading, our hearts must be open to Him to hear. He speaks in a still small voice, if we continue to ignore Him He will stop speaking to us.

Chapter 32

A LIGHT UNTO MY PATH, HIS BURDEN IS LIGHT.

A LIGHT UNTO MY PATH

"Thy word is a lamp unto my feet and a light unto my path" (Psalms 119:105)

The light in this scripture is speaking about spiritual illumination, by divine truth that comes from God only. The word is the only thing that will keep us secure in this life and lead us to eternal life. "And the Word was made flesh and dwelt among us (And we beheld His glory, the glory as of the only begotten of the Father,) full of grace and truth" (John 1:14). The Word was Jesus. "In Him was life; and the life was the light of men. And the light shinneth in darkness; and the darkness comprehened it not" (John 1:4–5). This light shined upon sinful men but they did not want to recieve spiritual illumination from the way, the truth, and the life. They would not recieve His gift of eternal life.

HIS BURDEN IS LIGHT

"Come unto me, all ye that labour and are heavy laden, and I will give you rest. Take my yoke upon you, and learn of me; for I am meek and lowly in heart: and ye shall find rest unto your souls. For my yoke is easy, and my burden is light." (Matthew 11:28–30).

There are times when we become weary, from carrying burdens too heavy for us. Burdens of sickness, poverty, worry, unbelief, family situations, and fear. When this happens the enemy can easily distracts us, causing us to see our problems as humongous. We lose our faith in God and don't see a way out. As we quiet our minds and remember that God is all powerful our faith will be renewed. He is bigger than any situation that may arise in our lives. When we go to Him He will give us rest. We work so hard from the yoke of men and recieve only monetary rewards, but Jesus wants to give us a reward of eternal life. Jesus says, take my yoke and learn of me. And what do we learn about Him? that He is meek (the meek shall inherit the earth), that He is lowly in heart (the humble are the greatest in the kingdom of heaven, they shall be exhalted, and shall recieve grace). (Matthew 18:4, 23:12, James 4:6). As we learn of Him, we will become like Him, because His yoke fits perfectly, and His burdens are light. He is the only one, who can give rest, to our weary souls.

Chapter 33

GREAT IS THY FAITH,
THE DAMASCUS ROAD EXPERIENCE,
JESUS TEMPTATIONS.

GREAT IS THY FAITH

"And behold a woman of Canaan came out of the same coasts, and cried unto Him, saying, have mercy on me, O Lord, thou Son of David, my daughter is grievously vexed with a devil. But He answered her not a word. And the disciples came and besought Him, saying, Send her away; for she crieth after us. But He answered and said, I am not sent but unto the lost sheep of the house of Israel. Then Jesus answered and said unto her, O woman, great is thy faith: be it unto thee even as thou wilt. And her daughter was made whole from that very hour." (Matthew 15:22, 23, 24, 28).

This woman of Canaan, had heard of the healings that Jesus had been performing. She went to Jesus with the faith that her daughter would be healed. This woman recieved her desire because she came bodly in faith and God is a merciful God. She cried out have mercy on me O Lord thou son of David. Jesus didn't answer her at this point, but I am sure she got His attention. He probally thought, this woman called me Lord. Finally, He said, I am not sent but unto the lost sheep of the house of Israel (meaning the Jews and she was Gentile). However this woman was persistant. When Jesus made that statement, she didn't turn away and say Lord I understand, she came and worshiped Him. To worship means to honour, and adore. I can imagine that this woman fell upon her knees and praised and adored the Lord. Then Jesus said, it is not meet to take the children's bread, and cast it to the dogs. (dogs was a name for Gentiles). I believe Jesus wanted to see, how bad she wanted to see her daughter healed. She answered Jesus and said, "Truth Lord yet the dogs eat of the crumbs which fall from the master's table". What a word! I believe the woman was saying I don't want all of the Jews blessings just a crumb will be enough to heal my daughter. When the woman spoke those words, Jesus could no longer keep her blessing from her. He said, "O woman great is thy faith; be it unto thee, even as thou wilt, and her daughter was made whole from that very hour. The woman's faith in Jesus gave her what she came for. "Without faith it is impossible to please Him: for he that cometh to God must believe that he is, and that he is a rewarder of them that diligently seek Him" (Hebrew 11:6). Do you desire anything so much that you will humble yourself, be ignored, and refused twice?

THE DAMASCUS ROAD EXPERIENCE

"And as he journed he came near Damascus: and suddenly there shined around him a light from heaven: And he fell to the earth, and heard a voice saying saying unto him, Saul, Saul, why persecuted thou me? And he said, who art thou Lord? And the Lord said, I am Jesus whom thou persecutest: it is hard for thee to kick against the pricks. And he trembling and astonished said, Lord, what will thou have me to do? And the Lord said unto him, arise, and go into the city, and it will be told thee what thou must do" (Acts 9:3–6).

What a great conversion experience Paul had! I believe Paul had such an a experience, because Paul needed to know, who was sending him. Paul would carry Jesus name before Jews, Gentiles, Kings, and would suffer, great things for the cause of Christ. When Jesus told Paul who He was, he said, Lord, what will thou have me to do. I don't know about you, but when I was converted I was only concerned, about what the Lord could do for me! Paul conversion was a true conversion because he called Jesus Lord. "No man can say that Jesus is lord except by the Holy Ghost" (I Corinthians 12:3). From that moment on Paul was not his own, he belonged to Jesus. Paul accepted his calling with all his heart. His life was never the same after that experience, neither the Church, or the world.

JESUS TEMPTATIONS

"Then was Jesus led up of the Spirit into the wilderness to be tempted of the devil" (Matthew 4:1).

Immediately after Jesus was baptized, He was led into the wilderness by the Holy Spirit. Many of us believe that when we are baptized all our trouble will be over, but this is not the true fact. The devil dosen't want to let go of us and this is when the trials and temptations began. Just as Jesus, the Son of God, was tempted we must be also. After Jesus had fasted forty days and forty nights satan came to Him. He knows our weakest point. He knew that Jesus was hungry, so he tempted by saying, "If thou be the Son of God, command that these stones be made bread". Jesus said, "It is written, Man shall not live by bread alone, but by every word that proceedeth out of the mouth of God" (Matthew 4:3.4). The devil always wants to put doubt in our minds, concerning who we are, and what we believe, as he did Eve in the Garden, when he said, "Ye shall not surely die" (Genesis 3:4). I believe Jesus fasted because He wanted us to have control over our appetite not just for food only, but for all the things of the world. Some of us believe if we miss one meal we are going to pass out, however, fasting is beneficial for the body, spirit and mind. Jesus over came all three of satan temptations by the word of God. His second temptation was: "If thou be the Son of God, cast thyself down: for it is written, He shall give his angels charge concerning thee: and in their hands they shall bear thee up, lest at any time thou dash thy foot against a stone. Jesus said, "It is written again, Thou shalt not tempt the Lord thy God". (Matthew 4: 6, 7). The third temptation was: "Again, the devil taketh Him up into an exceeding high mountain, and sheweth Him all the kingdoms of the world, and the glory of them; And saith unto Him, all these things will I give thee, if thou wilt fall down and worship me. Then saith Jesus unto him, Get thee hence, Satan: for it is written, Thou shalt worship the Lord thy God, and Him only shalt thou serve" (Matthew 4:8–10). Perhaps, the devil thought, that because Jesus, was so hungry, and weak He had forgotten who He was. The devil was thrown our of heaven, because he wanted to be worshiped, above God, and that is his desire today. Remember we can have the victory only through the word of God. Each time Jesus was tempted He said, "It is written". The devil knows the word, that is why he is working so furiously in these last days, because he knows he is a defeated foe and we are victorious in Christ Jesus!

Chapter 34

WALK IN NEWNESSS OF LIFE, THREE ANGLES MESSAGE

WALK IN NEWNESS OF LIFE

"Therefore we are buried with Him by baptism into death: that like as Christ was raised up from the dead by the glory of the Father, even so we should walk in newness of life. For if we have been planted together in the likeness of His death, we shall also in the likeness of His resurrection: Knowing this, that our old man is crucified with Him, that the body of sin might be destroyed. That henceforth we should not serve sin" (Romans 6:4–6).

When we were baptized, we died and were buried with Christ. Christ was raised to life by the glory of God the Father and if we shared in Jesus death by being baptized, we will be raised to life with Him. Baptism in of itself does not save us, it does not change the heart of a person. It is a step of obedience, and a symbol of the change, that has already taken place, by our trust being placed in the Lord. Baptism cannot make a person new, it is the transforming power of the Holy Spirit, that change the heart at conversion. Baptism does not necessairly make a person feel good, it is not a matter of feeling, but of faith and obedience. Baptism does not remove temptation. The devil is not through with you at baptism. However, Jesus will be with you. "There hath no temptation taken you but such as is common to man: but God is faithful, who will not suffer you to be tempted above that ye are able; but will with the temptation also make a way to escape, that ye may be able to bear it" (I Corinthians 10:13). Conversion must come before baptism, if not, baptism is meaningless.

THREE ANGELS MESSAGE

"And I saw another angel fly in the midst of heaven, having the everlasting gospel to preach unto them that dwell on the earth, and to every nation, and kindred, and tongue, and people. Saying with a loud voice, Fear God, and give glory to Him; for the hour of His judgment is come: and worship Him that made heaven, and earth, and the sea, and the fountains of waters. And there followed another angel, saying, Babylon is fallen, is fallen, that great city, because she made all nations drink of the wine of the wrath of her fornication. And the third angel followed them, saying with a loud voice, if any man worship the beast and his image, and receive his mark in his forehead, or in his hand , the same shall drink of the wine of the wrath of God, which is poured out without mixture into the cup of His indignation; and he shall be tormented with fire and brimstone in the presence of the holy angels, and in the presence of the Lamb" (Revelations 14:7–10).

The three angel's message stress the gospel, which make it plain that people are saved by faith and acceptance of Jesus Christ alone. Fear God means we should reverence and look upon Him with love, trust, and respect eager to obey His word. This keep us from evil. "By the fear of the lord men depart from evil" (Proverbs 16:6). We must give glory to God, We fulfill this command when we obey, praise, and thank God for His goodness to us. The hour of His judgement is come, this indicates that everyone is accountable to God, and it is a clear statement that judgement is now in session. Worship the creator, this command rejects idolatry of all kinds including self-worship and totally repudiates evolution. Many books, radio, tv, and talk shows overstress self-worth, which leads to self-worship. Our value can be found, only, in Jesus our creator. We worship the creator by keeping the sabbath day holy, the day that is a memorial of His creation. Saturday, the seventh day sabbath. The third angel's message warns people against worshipping the beast, and recieving the mark of the beast, in their forehead or hand.

Chapter 35

HE IS OUR GOD,
PRAY WITHOUT CEASING.

HE IS OUR GOD

"O come, let us worship and bow down: let us kneel before the Lord our maker. For He is our God; and we are the people of His pasture, and the sheep of His hand" (Psalms 95:6,7).

It seems as though for this generation, there is no time to set aside for the Lord. we are so caught up in the cares of this world, that we fail to understand, that worship, is what the christian walk is all about. When we worship God, we connect ourselves to Him, in such a way, that He is able to transform our lives. Worship is not about us, but about God. However, worship does benefit us, but it does so only, because we focus our attention on God. As we do, we are drawn closer to Him, and realize what God has given to us, in Christ Jesus. As we focus on Him, these thoughts awakens feelings of love for Him, and the outcome of this worship, gives us freedom from devotion to other things. It is a freedom to give affection to, and receive affection, from the one who loves us, more than anyone else ever could. God, the eternal, self-existent, uncreated one, Himself, the source and sustainer of all, is alone entitled to supreme reverence and worship.

PRAY WITHOUT CEASING

"Peter therefore was kept in prison: but prayer was made without ceasing of the church unto God for him" (Acts 12:5).

King Herod moved against some of the believers and killed the apostle James (John's brother). When Herod saw how much this pleased the Jewish leaders, he arrested Peter during the passover celebration. While Peter was kept in prison, the church was earnestly praying to God for him. "And when Herod would have brought him forth, the same night peter was sleeping between two soldiers, bound with two chains: and the keepers before the door kept the prison. And, behold, the angel of the Lord came upon him, and a light shined in the prison: and he smote Peter on the side, and raised him up, saying, Arise up quickly, And his chains fell off from his hands. And when Peter was come to himself, he said, Now I know of a surety, that the Lord hath sent his angel, and hath delivered me out of the hand of Herod, and from all the expectation of the people of the Jews" (Acts 12:6, 7, 11). Peter went to the home of Mary, mother of John Mark, where they were praying for him. He knocked at the door and Rhoda came to open the door, and saw that it was Peter. She was so excited, she forgot to open the door and let Peter in. She ran to tell the others. Finally, they opened the door, and he told them what had happened, they were astonished! Isn't that just like christians, we pray and when God answers our prayer we are suprised. However, the word says "The effectual fervent prayer of a righteous man availeth much" (James 5:16).

Chapter 36

HE HAS CHOSEN US, EXTRAVAGANT LOVE.

HE HAS CHOSEN US

"According as He hath chosen us in Him before the foundation of the world, that we should be holy and without blame before Him in love. Having predestinated us unto the adoption of children by Jesus Christ to Himself, according to the good pleasure of His will" (Ephesians 1:4, 5).

Chosen in Christ is an acknowledgment of the divine provision, which provided salvation for the whole world but made effective only to those who claimed it for themselves. Predestination simply means that it is God's will that salvation be available to all. Salvation and eternal life are made availabe to all as a gift of God in Jesus, but only "Whoever believes in Him" shall be saved. It is not that God choose some and rejects others, instead, it's that those who have accepted what Christ has done for them have simply fulfilled what was originally planned for them from the start. " The Lord is not slack concerning His promise, as some men count slackness; but is longsuffering to us-ward, not willing that any should perish, but that all should come to repenance" (II Peter 3:9). God does not determine who will accept that salvation and who will not. Acceptance is entirely dependant on human choice. God's adoption of us as His children is dependant on His redemptive plan carried out through His son on the cross. Our sins are forgiven through the blood of Jesus shed on the cross. Without that shed blood, without a sinless saviour dying for the sins of the world, there is no forgiveness and no redemption. Jesus blood paid the penalty for our sins. When we accept that substitutionary death, our sins are forgiven and we become eligible for the heavenly inheritance, sealed and made sure by the gift of the Holy Spirit. Take away the cross, and we have no forgiviness, no salvation, no promise, and no sealing of the Holy Spirit. (*Quartely* Oct.–Dec. p. 32 2005).

EXTRAVAGANT LOVE

"Then took Mary a pound of ointment of spikenard, very costly, and antointed the feet of Jesus, and wiped His feet with her hair: and the house filled with the odour of the ointment. Then saith one of his disciples, Judas Iscariot, Simon's son, which should betray Him, Why was not this ointment sold for three hundred pence, and given to the poor? Then said Jesus, Let her alone: against the day of my burying hath she kept this. For the poor always ye have with you; but me ye have not always" (John 12:3–5, 7,8,).

Judas complained, because he was a thief, and was only concerned about money for himself. The scripture says this ointment was very costly. However, Mary loved Jesus so much, that she didn't care about spending lots of money for Jesus. Mary showed "Extravagant Love" for Jesus. She even wiped His feet with her hair. When we see the word extravagent we think of spending money excessively, immoderate or wasteful in use of resources, exorbitant; costing much, exceeding normal restraint or sense, unreasonable; absurd. I would like to use the definition for what Mary did as "Exceeding normal restraint" Mary loved Jesus so much, that she did what was not normally done; she wanted to show Jesus and the people around her just how much she really loved Jesus. Do you have extravagant love for Jesus? When was the last time you went out and did something extravagant for Him? I hang my head in shame, when I think about how little I have done to show my love for Him. Jesus showed extravagant love for us, in His death on the cross, He gave His life. "And being found in fashion as a man, He humbled Himself, and became obedient unto death, even the death of the cross" (Philippians 2:8). That's what I call extravagant love! So what's my problem? What's keeping me from showing extravagant love?

Chapter 37

SALVATION IS NEAR, HEAVEN.

SALVATION IS NEAR

"And that, knowing the time, that now it is high time to awake out of sleep: for now is our salvation nearer than when we believed" (Roman 13:11).

We are going through all the right motions, saying all the right words but the word says, "This people draweth nigh unto me with their mouth, and honoureth me with their lips; but their heart is far from me" (Matthew 15:8). The truth is we are dying of thrist for contact with the living God. Although many of us, continue to drag ourselves to church, week in and week out, underneath we are parched and shriveled. The effects of spiritual thirst, are unmistakable, and painful. The hard hearts, the sharp tongues, the long pinched faces, of those who claim to be redeemed, and the absence of young people, tell the true story. These are symptoms that only Jesus can cure. It's time to pray. I know that we pray, but is it the kind of prayer that bring about real and lasting changes? the prayer that cause us, to see ourselves as we really are, that help us admit how much we need Jesus? The kind of prayer we need is: "If my people, who are called by my name, will humble themselves and pray and seek my face and turn from their wicked ways, then will I hear from heaven and will forgive their sin and heal their land" (II Chronicles 7:14). When God heals our land, we will wake from our sleep, and know that not only, is our salvation nearer than we believe; but also the salvation of our family, and our neighbour. This healing will cause us to have a burning desire to "Go Ye therefore, and teach all nations baptizing them in the name of the Father and of the Son and of the Holy Ghost Teaching them to observe all things whatsoever I have commanded you: and lo, I am with you alway, even unto the end of the world" (Matthew 28:19, 20). "It is high time to wake out of sleep". His favour will be upon us as we "Go".

HEAVEN

"And I saw a new heaven and a new earth: for the first heaven and the first earth were passed away; and there was no more sea. And I John saw the Holy City, New Jerusalem, coming down from God out of heaven, prepared as a bride adorned for her husband" (Revelation 21:1, 2).

John in his vision is telling us about the new heaven and earth that he saw. John let's us know that this old earth that we live on now will be destroyed and will be made beautiful. The Holy City, New Jerusalem, will come down from heaven to earth. All the righteous will have a home in this city. God will dwell with us. "And I heard a great voice out of heaven saying, Behold, the tabernacle of God is with men, and He will dwell with them, and they shall be His people, and God Himself shall be with them, and be their God. And God shall wipe away all tears from their eyes; and there shall be no more death, neither sorrow, nor crying, neither shall there be any more pain: for the former things are passed away" (Revelation 21:3, 4) How wonderful that will be! no more tear, no more death, neither sorrow, nor pain. "And the city had no need of the sun, neither of the moon, to shine in it; for the glory of God did lighten it, and the Lamb is the light thereof" (Revelation 21:23). "In the midst of the street of it, and on either side of river, was there the tree of life, which bare twelve manner of fruits, and yielded her fruit every month: and the leaves of the tree were for the healing of the nations" (Revelation 22:2). "And many false prophets shall rise, and shall deceive many, And because iniquity shall abound, the love of many shall wax cold. But he that shall endure unto the end, the same shall be saved" (Matthew 24:11–13). Only those that endure until the end will spend eternity with the Lord. I want to be there, do you? I am looking foward to heaven, because Jesus will be there, my blessed saviour.

We'd love to have you download our catalog of titles we publish at:

www.TEACHServices.com

or write or email us your thoughts, reactions, or criticism about this or any other book we publish at:

TEACH Services, Inc.
254 Donovan Road
Brushton, NY 12916

info@TEACHServices.com

or you may call us at:

518/358-3494